THE HEALTH HAZARD

PRAISE FOR **THE HEALTH HAZARD**

This book is a highly practical manual for not just surviving but learning to flourish in those emotionally hazardous environments all too often found in our health and social care sectors. We all know these places, where unrealistic demands and conflicts lead on to exhaustion, loss of belief and purpose and feelings of defeat, failure and cynicism all covered under the general label "Burnout".

Alison writes vividly and with great candour about her personal experiences and struggles. She offers a down-to-earth roadmap for evading and escaping the traps of toxic work, and instead finding a sustainable personal and family life alongside taking social responsibility for change.

Her book contains a rich range of reflections, techniques and planning tools from "baby steps" and "tiny habits" to practices of mindfulness, breathing and gratitude. All are described with a light touch that makes change feel like a realistic everyday possibility. The book is refreshing and the opposite of overwhelming.

I congratulate Alison on her ability to pull together so many ideas and tools so brilliantly. Even more I salute her courage, openness and generosity in writing this book.

**ONELLA STAGOLL OAM, MSC (COLUMBIA UNIVERSITY),
FOUNDING CEO, BREASTSCREEN VICTORIA**

Alison is spot on as she thoughtfully unpacks all the factors that can lead to burnout for so many of us in this sector as we push ever onward to change outcomes, make a difference or better our communities. The hamster wheel goes faster and faster and somehow we are powerless to know how to stop, get off and restart. In fact, it seems that this is simply our lot, as we have chosen this career. Read with eyes wide open, her simple yet transformational strategies enable you to get up from face down and to repair and refill your 'bucket'. Alison guides you step by step to make changes that will not only have an impact on you, but those around you at home and at work, as you personally feel the benefits of change, and model those healthy behaviours to others.

ELISABETH BAUGH, CEO, OVARIAN CANCER CANADA AND CHAIR, WORLD OVARIAN CANCER COALITION

This is an incredibly important and timely book, for two reasons. Firstly Alison Coughlan shines the light on what was already a crisis in the health and social sector pre-COVID19, and is now an order of magnitude worse around the world. Burnout. (And no, the irony isn't lost on Alison that a sector that has compassion at its core is dangerously lacking in self care). Secondly this book shows us, in simple, powerful terms, what to do about it. Compulsory reading for anyone who works in or cares about this sector.

PETER COOK, AUTHOR OF MULTIPLE BOOKS INCLUDING IMPLEMENT!

Big Ben was definitely ringing his bell for me throughout this book!

In The Health Hazard, Alison explores the world of the not-for-profit and health areas – the multiple, complex issues, the dedication, guilt, selflessness, passion, persistence, frustration, never-enough-time and exhaustion that encircles us.

She has done this with remarkable candour, honestly admitting to her own burnout and encouraging the reader to evaluate their own professional and private lives in order to avoid this themselves.

The issues raised are rarely discussed so openly within our sector. When faced with overwhelming challenges, we feel we have no other choice but to push on, producing outstanding results and being the perfect high-achieving professional - after all, we care for others and the world needs us!

What Alison's book does is acknowledge the very real problems we face – and, importantly, offer tangible strategies for our ongoing recovery. In this time of COVID, her messages and tips have never been more relevant.

LYN SWINBURNE AO, FOUNDER, BREAST CANCER NETWORK AUSTRALIA, BOARD CHAIR, THE ROYAL WOMEN'S HOSPITAL

I don't know anyone who hasn't experienced what is outlined in Alison's book, it was so heartening for me to read it and to see practical tools that can be used to avoid experiencing burnout and to overcome it!

CALANEET BALAS, PRESIDENT AND CEO, THE ALS ASSOCIATION (USA) AND CHAIR, INTERNATIONAL ALLIANCE OF ALS/MND ASSOCIATIONS

You won't find any fluff in this book. Alison shares with transparency and grit how she wrestled with burnout and got her life back. If you're struggling with burnout and want to do something about it, sit down with this book, roll up your sleeves, and put together a plan.

DAN DIAMOND MD, PRINCIPAL, NOGGINSTORM INC
WWW.DANDIAMONDMD.COM

The stress of our daily lives is taking its toll – we are busier than ever, always connected and the lines between work and life are becoming increasingly blurred. For those of us in purpose-driven roles our response is to just keep pushing through - to keep trying harder – and over time this can take a toll on our health and our relationships and ultimately lead to burnout. Alison Coughlan has experienced burnout first hand and in her book shares her experiences and the lessons she's learnt along her journey. It's a great read, written from the heart, that helps us understand the drivers of burnout and importantly the practical changes we can make to live our best lives both at work and at home.

ASSOCIATE PROFESSOR TONY WALKER, ASM, FACPARA,
CHIEF EXECUTIVE OFFICER, AMBULANCE VICTORIA

The Health Hazard
Copyright © 2021 by Alison Coughlan
All rights reserved.

Published by Grammar Factory Publishing, an imprint of MacMillan Company Limited.

No part of this book may be used or reproduced in any manner whatsoever without the prior written permission of the author, except in the case of brief passages quoted in a book review or article. All enquiries should be made to the author.

Grammar Factory Publishing
MacMillan Company Limited
25 Telegram Mews, 39th Floor, Suite 3906
Toronto, Ontario, Canada
M5V 3Z1

www.grammarfactory.com

Coughlan, Alison–
The Health Hazard: Take Control, Restore Wellbeing and Optimise Impact / Alison Coughlan.

Paperback ISBN 978-1-989737-18-7
eBook ISBN 978-1-989737-19-4

    1. BUS107000 BUSINESS & ECONOMICS / Personal Success. 2. SEL027000 SELF-HELP / Personal Growth / Success. 3. SEL044000 SELF-HELP / Self-Management / General.

Production Credits
Printed in Australia by IngramSpark
Cover design by Designerbility
Interior layout design by Dania Zafar
Book production and editorial services by Grammar Factory Publishing

Grammar Factory's Carbon Neutral Publishing Commitment
From January 1st, 2020 onwards, Grammar Factory Publishing is proud to be neutralizing the carbon footprint of all printed copies of its authors' books printed by or ordered directly through Grammar Factory or its affiliated companies through the purchase of Gold Standard-Certified International Offsets.

Disclaimer
The material in this publication is of the nature of general comment only and does not represent professional advice. It is not intended to provide specific guidance for particular circumstances, and it should not be relied on as the basis for any decision to take action or not take action on any matter which it covers. Readers should obtain professional advice where appropriate, before making any such decision. To the maximum extent permitted by law, the author and publisher disclaim all responsibility and liability to any person, arising directly or indirectly from any person taking or not taking action based on the information in this publication.

THE HEALTH HAZARD

TAKE CONTROL, RESTORE
WELLBEING AND OPTIMISE IMPACT

ALISON COUGHLAN

CONTENTS

About the Author — xi
Dedication — xiii

Part 1: A Sustained State of Crisis We Have Normalised — 1
Introduction — 3
Chapter 1: It's Time to Take Control, and it Starts With You — 33

Part 2: Getting Practical and Zooming in on You — 55
Chapter 2: Insight: Face Your Truth — 59
Chapter 3: Mindset: Enable Change — 89
Chapter 4: Energy: Build Your Reserves — 133

Part 3: Commit to You and Plan for Your Success — 177
Chapter 5: Pulling Together Your Personal Impact Plan — 179
Conclusion: My Hopes for You — 189

Endnotes — 193

ABOUT THE AUTHOR

Alison Coughlan, BSc (Hons), MPH, is a speaker, author, mentor and facilitator who builds the capabilities of people working in the health and social sectors. People who are motivated to make a difference in the lives of others through their work in direct and indirect roles seeking to provide care, relief and hope, prevent ill health and suffering, and reduce inequalities and disadvantage.

Alison's practice is grounded in a life-long desire to *make a difference* and is informed by more than twenty-five years' experience in the health and social sectors. Alison has had the privilege of working at a state, national and global level with more than seventy-five organisations as a researcher, policy maker, advocate, leader, consultant and board director.

Alison's work also draws on her personal experience of reaching, sustaining and recovering from burnout, after which she charted a new, more fulfilling and sustainable path for her work and her life.

For the rest of Alison's career, she intends to share what she has learnt with others to help them optimise the impact they make and, in so doing, do their best work *and* live their best life.

Alison is a proud mum of three daughters and lives in Victoria, Australia.

alisoncoughlan.com
Facebook.com/AlisonCoughlanInc
Twitter: @CoughlanAlison

DEDICATION

This book is dedicated to Alexandra, Georgia and Sophie. Being your mum is the greatest role I will ever take on. You are my inspiration and, through you, I source a wellspring of courage, determination, sheer grit, fierceness and daring.

Nick, my great love. You see me, challenge me and believe in me, and bring so much joy into my life (being hilarious will do that!). With you, my girls, and the beautiful Caitie and Em, I am truly living a life that dreams are made of.

I just pinched myself.

It's real.

PART I

A SUSTAINED STATE OF CRISIS WE HAVE NORMALISED

In Part 1, the scene is set through exploring the insidious and devastating problem of burnout in the health and social sector workforce. We'll look at its prevalence, causes and consequences, and identify some of the masks that we might wear when we live and work with the pall of burnout hanging over us in our daily lives.

We'll consider the irony that, while our sector has compassion at its core, there can be a lack of compassion for ourselves, which can place us at increased risk of decline. We'll dig into issues of compassion for the self and for others. Finally, we'll explore a new way of looking at compassion to create a space in which we can claim control over ourselves and our lives, charting a new and different course in work *and* in life.

INTRODUCTION

Burnout: the reduction of a fuel or substance to nothing through use or combustion.[1]

In the health and social sectors, our business is about creating change. Change in the life of individuals, families, communities and society through our spectrum of work across all stages of life, with people from all walks of life.

We apply our skills (technical and interpersonal) to provide care, relief and hope, and to prevent ill health and suffering. This may occur in a variety of ways. In direct frontline roles as allied health professionals, nurses and doctors. Indirectly, through research into ways to reduce the burden of ill health and social disadvantage. As champions in the charity sector who advocate addressing gaps in the system and providing needed responses to unmet needs. As leaders, policy makers and change makers across the many parts of these sectors.

The choice to work in the health or social sectors is often associated with a passionate personal drive – a sense of vocation, even. I like to call this 'purpose-driven work'. As human beings, we

As human beings, we are fundamentally makers of meaning. When we engage in work that is intrinsically linked to our core purpose, it can bring great fulfilment and meaning to our lives. However, as we go about this work, the passion and heart that we put into it, that are essential to our effectiveness, also put us at risk.

are fundamentally makers of meaning. When we engage in work that is intrinsically linked to our core purpose, it can bring great fulfilment and meaning to our lives. However, as we go about this work, the passion and heart that we put into it, that are essential to our effectiveness, also put us at risk.

At risk of what? Burnout.

THE BURNOUT PROBLEM OF PURPOSE-DRIVEN WORK

What we witness, and the emotions that we feel as we go about our purpose-driven work, can drain us of our energy and wellbeing. The separation between work and the rest of our life can blur. Our work can impact our life both positively and negatively. And our personal challenges can also impact our capacity to sustain the energy and wellbeing we need for our work.

Beyond just sustaining ourselves, we can become depleted and, at worst, reduced to nothing – as the literal definition of burnout suggests.

But despite warning signs – if we notice them – we often just keep on going, putting our own needs aside as we continue to turn up to serve our families, our communities and the beneficiaries of our work.

All the while, we are suffering ourselves.

THE ENDLESS CYCLE OF SUFFERING: IN THE INDIVIDUAL AND IN ORGANISATIONS

As the demands and pressures of your work grow or simply remain stubbornly relentless, and your wellbeing and stamina wane, you may search for silver bullets. Solutions that will bring ease and increase impact. You lobby for additional resources as the funding and people power available is completely inadequate to achieve the goals set for your organisation or for you personally. Ambitious, inspired and laudable goals, sure, but always too many priorities and not enough time, energy and resources to adequately address them. So you are set up for the relentless challenge where constant striving is business as usual, without respite. You become increasingly frustrated and disenfranchised when, despite your best efforts, you feel like you are not making meaningful progress. You – or others who you work with – are just not okay. Going to work each day feels like an increasingly heavy burden to carry.

You may step on to the hamster wheel. The hamster wheel refers to the concept of running in circles but never making progress that is meaningful. Guided by the sense that motion is the most important thing, saying to yourself over and over, 'I just need to keep going.' And so, you peddle away on that wheel, keep on keeping on, maintaining a frenetic pace at times as you seek to do more and be more. All the while you are further depleting your energy, draining your reserves and decreasing your resilience.

When caught on the hamster wheel, it's not hard to see how you can gradually lose connection to the meaning and purpose that guided your choice of work in the first place. When this plays

INTRODUCTION | 7

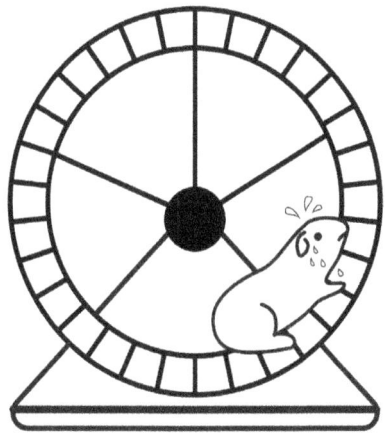

itself out in workplaces where multiple people are on that wheel, our workplace cultures can take a hit. You may not feel seen or heard or valued despite the incredible lengths you are going to. Difficult emotions and unhealthy behaviours can creep into your own experience and that of others who you work with. Perhaps there's people you consider are not pulling their weight. Maybe others who look at the clock and raise their eyebrows every time you race out the door to pick up the kids before childcare closes. Judgement, disapproval, resentment, blame – leading to battle lines being drawn and previously effective, productive relationships becoming strained.

Organisations created to deliver social impact can become toxic, inefficient and ineffective – and the limited resources that are available are then spread even more thinly as time, energy and money are invested in dealing with performance issues, conflict in the workplace, and responding to a high level of staff disconnection and apathy, as well as growing absenteeism and, inevitably, staff turnover.

This work of dealing with crises, putting out fires, managing conflict and performance, and filling the gaps left by absenteeism – or what can feel like a constant stream of vacancies to be filled by departing employees – feels like a further drain on your energy and wellbeing.

And it's really frustrating.

You want to be focused on the 'real work', the 'important work', the delivery of the organisation's mission – and yet you feel diverted into managing crises that are not adding value or contributing to meaningful change. This creates a further divide between your sense of purpose, your passion and your drive, and what you are finding yourself doing.

This can lead you on the slow and insidious path to burnout.

When burnout starts to take its toll, you disconnect, retreat, numb the pain and fill the void. You might escape into one of the many addictions that are available to us in our modern lives – our electronic devices, binge-watching an ever-increasing array of entertainment, having a drink or two in the evening after work, or consuming comfort food. The list goes on. When you take these steps, you might feel some relief for a time. But at some point, the coping strategies that you originally turned to as something to help you feel better have the potential to further compromise your health, deteriorate your wellbeing and perpetuate your decline.

If you are not okay, there are no silver bullets or quick fixes you can implement that are going to help you personally – or that will assist you in achieving your goals or sustaining your efforts.

It is only through a focus on your wellbeing – and working to get yourself to a place where your energy and wellbeing are optimised – that you will be able to learn and grow, to take risks, to face challenges, and to be resilient when crises occur. In order to do this, you *must* come first.

How do I know this?

I've lived it – and I learnt the hard way that we can't serve those we care for if we don't carve out an easier path for ourselves first.

WHY I WROTE THIS BOOK

In the past six years, I have gone from being face down to living a life so wonderful that I pinch myself regularly to check that it is actually real. I use the term 'face down' to describe the state in which I found myself in early 2015 when the full force of burnout had taken a hefty toll on me. I was absolutely and utterly exhausted. I was incredibly emotional, highly sensitive, and I felt a heavy pall of despair. Sometimes I just felt numb.

I wondered if I would ever actually recover and wondered what lay ahead for me. I certainly didn't even really feel like myself anymore. It felt like I had slowly slipped away over many years without my conscious awareness, and I found myself at a point where I didn't trust myself and wondered whether I was up to doing anything at all. My professional and personal confidence was knocked with the experiences I'd had, and with the many changes I'd made in my career in response to challenges at work and challenges at home.

With an open heart, I share in this book what I have discovered along the way – from the starting point of face down through a long, slow process of recovery and, later, to carving a new path for my work and for my life. Everything in this book reflects strategies I have tried out and found helpful.

And here's the thing: I *know* I'm not alone. I first spoke about burnout in 2014 when I was asked to give a keynote address at a Women in Leadership Summit. At the time, I was the CEO of Ovarian Cancer Australia and I was charged with speaking on the topic of 'Planning your next: Reaching senior leadership level'. The eager audience of women were poised with pens and notepads, expecting to hear me extol the seven tips to securing their first C-level role or the ten key ingredients to their career success.

They didn't quite get what they bargained for. Instead, I told them the truth of my story and started with a message along the lines of, 'While I would like to share with you the golden key or keys that will unlock the door to your career progression, my path has been a little more like this...' Cue slide with broken wooden sign that says: 'Caution: Rough Road Ahead'.

I shared the true, warts-and-all story of my path through my career to that point.

I talked about the challenges I faced and critical decisions, both personal and professional, that I made along the way. I spoke of doing a juggling act ... while tap dancing ... and spinning plates ... in heels. Of trying to do and be everything that all the people in my life wanted and needed me to be. I spoke of getting it right some of the time and not feeling like I was doing anything terribly

well most of the time. I spoke of struggles and difficult choices and experiences of burnout.

Despite many challenges I'd faced in my career and life, I was the CEO of a national charity. We had developed an incredible visionary strategy, I had built an extraordinary team, and we were embarking on the development of a national action plan for ovarian cancer research – we were talking the talk and we were walking the walk. We were working with and on behalf of incredible women affected by this devastating disease. We were growing national awareness and support for the cause, and I had become involved in the global ovarian cancer movement. I had reconnected the organisation with the intentions of our founder, Sheila Lee, and her vision to not just tinker around the edges but truly make a difference in the survival outcomes for women.

And I was a mother of three beautiful girls, so I had successfully juggled a career and family life to that point. 'Yay me', right? So in that talk, I provided my advice about work and life, some tips, and messages of hope for those who might have felt that they were struggling themselves.

Now this is where it gets really interesting.

The response from the audience was not what I was expecting. Now, I'm not sure what I really expected, but I can distinctly remember thinking to myself, as I prepared my presentation, that I must actually be mad. I was outing myself here as not being okay and I thought perhaps this could either be a career-limiting step or at least might mean that any future invitations to speak may be few and far between.

So, the response?

I was approached by several women after the talk, and there were hugs and there were tears. They were grateful that I had chosen to share my story, warts and all, and they were so, so relieved. I've since spoken more freely about my experiences without the same sense of trepidation (well, maybe a little). Each time, without fail, what I say strikes a chord with the audience. There are usually tears and, often, sighs of relief.

What was this sense of relief about?

> *That they are not alone in their struggles.*

> *That I am real and flawed, just like them.*

That I have recovered from burnout, and that I am doing good work and making an impact, against the odds.

That maybe they can be okay too, and, beyond that, that they'd go to the places they wanted to go and perhaps even find an easier path to get there.

These experiences and lessons I have now embedded into my mentoring programs, and I have freely and openly shared what I have learnt with clients and colleagues. My hope is that my story and lessons learnt might help to pave a better and easier path forward for others. And I decided to write this book with the same intention in mind.

So, as I've done many times to help others, let me share with you my story...

MY STORY

Since I was a little girl, I can remember thinking, 'I am going to make a difference.' This passion and the drive that goes with it have guided the choices I have made throughout my education and my career in the 'for-purpose' sector.

I started my career as an immunology researcher working in transplantation and, later, HIV research in the early 1990s. Fuelled by a desire to be closer to the 'coal face', I completed further study in public health in my mid-twenties. All of my career has been in the health and social sectors, and I have had the privilege of taking on a whole range of roles in research, policy, quality improvement, program evaluation, consultation, training, consumer engagement, and in service and role redesign.

My leadership experience dates back to 2000 and I have held a series of management, executive and governance roles at state, national and global levels in government and non-government organisations. At the time of writing, I have run a small business for twelve years, from 2004 to 2010 and again since 2015. My clients are individuals and organisations in the health and social sectors, and, these days, my work is primarily as a consultant, teacher, mentor and facilitator.

At the time I gave that speech in 2014, I had worked for more than twenty years and I was making a difference. Tick! Colleagues and mentors would laud my efforts and the transformational change I was leading. They would describe me as inspirational and amazing, like a superwoman. They would say that they didn't know how I managed to do it all.

But I had a problem.

I was not okay – and I hadn't been okay for years.

I wasn't looking after myself. I was withdrawing and disconnecting. And I was oh, oh, so tired. I was barely holding it together – and I secretly wondered how much longer I could go on.

It turns out that it would only be a matter of time before I had my 'face down' moment, as the full force of burnout took its toll on me.

Thinking back, I first recall using the term 'burnout' after the birth of my third child in 2008. I found myself struggling to sustain my energy, looking after a baby and her two older sisters while running a consultancy business that was the only source of income for our family. In my early years in business, I completed almost 100 assignments for more than sixty organisations. I worked late into the night after my children were in bed and then would get up very early in the morning to get more work done before they awoke. I was chronically sleep deprived for years and years, and I routinely missed weekends and holidays as I kept striving to meet the needs of my clients and to make ends meet. The business had grown in the years prior and we had a team – so I could feel the growing weight of the responsibility of supporting multiple families, not just my own.

My second experience that I would call burnout was when I was working back in the health sector (in a real job!), and I experienced passively and overtly aggressive behaviour from a team member towards me that affected me profoundly.

When I reflect back on these times in my life, the words that come to mind are that I 'hit the deck'. I was highly emotional, I felt very vulnerable and wobbly (literally, like my knees might give way at times), and I became increasingly unsure of myself and worried about where I was at. At the same time, I also felt great pressure imposed by myself and by others. Personally, I needed to pull myself together because I needed to keep going. My financial situation was such that, if I didn't, there would be potentially significant consequences for my family. Professionally, people were suffering – we had no time to lose. We had to keep striving, keep pushing, keep going.

So, I kept going, and kept peddling on that hamster wheel. When I felt like I'd fallen off, I'd lick my wounds, dust myself off, and hop right back on. Sometimes this would happen after reinventing myself in some way, shifting my direction, or changing roles.

The hamster wheel became my refuge. When I was on the wheel, I was working hard, trying to be everything for everyone – and that felt like the right thing to do. Because it wasn't about me, right?

As a result, however, my energy and wellbeing had been slowly depleting over the years, and had reached dangerously low levels. Despite what I was achieving or what people saw on the outside, I was only just getting by.

This felt like a secret that I must not share and that people couldn't know. Otherwise, what would they then think of me? Would clients and team members lose their confidence in me? Would being open about what was happening to me affect my reputation? I just needed to keep running on that hamster wheel...

With the benefit of hindsight, and the wisdom, gentle encouragement and guidance of health professionals, I can now clearly see my struggle with burnout and how it emerged over time. I can see the long, slow decline in my energy and wellbeing over many years, and I can see multiple acute episodes of burnout where my resilience was low and a crisis would knock me down. As it turns out, I managed to live with sustained burnout for more than a decade before my final wake-up call.

At the time I gave that speech in 2014, I can see now that I was running on very close to empty. My resilience was low, and all that was needed was for another crisis to occur and I was at serious risk of falling off that hamster wheel. And that's exactly what happened. Another protracted and incredibly challenging period professionally ended in me leaving an organisation that I had helped to transform and grow, a wonderful team I had built, and the community we served and that I cared very deeply for. It was a very distressing time for me and, this time, when I came off the hamster wheel, there was no bouncing back.

This was my face down moment. I had a big problem and it was a matter of survival. I needed to be mentally and physically well enough to provide for my family. That included both earning a living to pay the bills but also providing the support, nurturing, love and care that they needed. I dearly wanted to provide all this but, at the time, felt unable to. This was my ground zero – and it was a terrifying and really confusing place to be. I was out of work, I was out of energy, I was desperately sad, I was out of confidence and I was out of ideas.

MY RECOVERY

My story of recovery doesn't start with a dramatic declaration of self-compassion. No light bulb moment with angels bursting into song as I committed to looking after myself once and for all as a new life philosophy.

It started from a place of need.

Basic need.

To care for my family.

To provide for my family.

If I wasn't okay, we weren't okay.

I needed to be okay.

And I wasn't.

The only possible way was up from that point.

If I stayed where I was or if I even went lower, I would be risking everything.

I had to recover.

Burnout could not be an option for me.

Not anymore.

And not ever again.

I had to choose to put myself first because that was the only way I could be of service to others.

Being in service was my link to purpose – and this realisation became the starting place for my recovery.

When I was face down, I hadn't fully faced the truth of my life, so I didn't have the insight, mindset and energy needed to reclaim myself and my life. I realised it was time for me to up the ante on self-compassion, to be 100 per cent responsible for myself and for my choices, and to stop giving that power to others. I faced the truth of my life and dared myself to chart a new course... And one moment, one breath, one minute, one hour, one day at a time, in small steps and in giant leaps, that's exactly what I did.

As soon as I started on this path, I could feel shifts and changes, and, along the way, I started to feel a little more daring.

I dared to believe that life didn't have to be so bloody hard.

I dared to believe that, if I could be well and live well, that my family would be able to as well.

I dared myself to be my best self, do my best work and live my best life.

I dared to create a thriving business that was aligned with my values, and that gave me the flexibility needed to be there for my family and take care of my wellbeing.

I dared to believe that I was enough, just the way I was. That I could even celebrate my inner superhero – a wholehearted disrupter who wears her heart on her sleeve, and who challenges herself and others to strive to be their best selves and do their best work.

I dared to take risks and to make mistakes – and to even forgive myself when I did. To know that I always had done the very best I could.

I dared to recapture dreams that I had long since dispensed with.

I even dared to find great love.

And I dared to attempt to believe that I was even worthy of all of this (and eventually, I actually believed it!).

The choices I made paid off. So did the hard work I invested in my recovery and in finding a path forward that was true to myself, and sticking to that path and never giving up, despite times when I really wanted to. My reward for all that pain was to go from face down to truly being able to say that today, I live a remarkable life of my own design. A life that continues to evolve in wonderful ways and that I expect will do so for the rest of my life.

THE LESSONS IN THIS BOOK

In this book, I'll share with you the many strategies that I found helpful as I charted my course from sustained burnout to doing my best work *and* living my best life. Everything in this book reflects something that I discovered as I sought advice from professionals, friends and family – and as I consumed copious amounts of information on burnout in many different forms. If there was something that could possibly help me, I was going to give it a shot, as I had nothing to lose and *everything* to gain.

These tried and tested methods are still in my toolkit. Some of them I practise most days. Some of them I turn to when I need a reset, or when I'm working through a challenging time. Just having the toolkit, and access to all of these tools that have been beneficial to me, gives me a sense of security and makes me feel at ease.

I know what I need to do if I'm not okay.

And I know it works.

And I don't hesitate to step up my efforts to focus on my energy and wellbeing when I need to.

Because burnout is a part of my past, not my present or my future.

While reading this book, I encourage you to play a game of Truth *and* Dare (not Truth or Dare – *and*). I'll share with an open heart what I have learnt from facing the truth of my life *and* from daring to chart a different course – and I invite you to do the same. This book will provide you with a step-by-step guide that shows you how to move away from a life full of stress, worry, frustration and struggle to a life that is more joyful – and in which you no longer fear that a day will come when you just won't be able to do this anymore.

This book is about putting yourself first (yes!), and doing so by developing insight, shifting your mindset, and building your energy reserves so you have the fuel to go the distance. And, most importantly, it is about seizing your own power, and taking control of your work and your life.

Choose to invest in you. Dedicate some of your precious time and energy to reading this book while letting your guard down (even if only with yourself). Dare to believe that it all doesn't have to be so hard. Follow the process laid out in this book, and think of the work you'll do while reading as a critical investment in you. In so doing, you will create a clear, personalised plan that will take you forward, helping you achieve greater reach and impact through your important purpose-driven work — without that being at the expense of your energy, your wellbeing and your life.

I hope that there's something in these pages that resonates with you — and, of course, I hope you get some benefits from reading them.

You'll find a mix of stories reflecting a composite of many anecdotes, experiences and observations I have made over time. They reflect key themes relating to the experience and manifestations of burnout, but they are fictional.

There are also some key statistics and facts about burnout spread throughout the book to shine a light on this insidious and devastating problem facing our health and social sectors, and why we need to address this now.

So, take a step forward onto a path that will lead you to greater wellbeing, meaning and joy, knowing that you are not alone.

What do you have to lose?

What could you gain?

You might even surprise yourself.

Go on, I dare you!

BURNOUT FACTS #1

AN INSIDIOUS PROBLEM

'Uh, Houston, we've had a problem here.'

These simple words have become an iconic, much-quoted, and sometimes misquoted, saying. It was Jack Swigert and then Jim Lovell who said these words as part of a radio transmission to NASA Mission Control during the Apollo 13 space mission. The transmission came after an explosion and a rupture in an oxygen tank.[2]

This story reflects a careful, highly engineered process that was in place well before the space shuttle launched in 1970. The incident was a potential disaster. While the astronauts' goal to land on the Moon did not eventuate, they returned home safely, so the mission was officially classified as a 'successful failure'.

In the Apollo 13 space mission, we see extensive preparation, training, development of supportive infrastructure, monitoring of progress, initiation of control procedures, and decision-making in response to a crisis situation. This enabled a disaster to be averted and lives to be saved.

Now, let's contrast the Apollo 13 story with the common path to burnout in the health and social sectors. No one would argue that there are no inherent risks to our wellbeing when we take on a career in these sectors. In fact, burnout was first described in 1974 as a phenomenon observed in healthcare workers.[3]

The statistics on stress, fatigue and burnout are clear – and they are alarming. We have tools to measure burnout, to track and monitor it, to identify warning signs and problems in an individual or team early, and to take remedial action. We are educated from early in our career about the importance of self-care, constantly being reminded that we need to manage our stress and consider our wellbeing. And yet, all too often, we don't.

There is a true disconnect between our knowledge and our behaviour – as individuals, in teams, in workplaces and across the sectors as a whole. We have normalised stress, constraint, demands, distress, fatigue and our prevailing culture of busyness. We quickly avert our attention from one problem to another, numb our feelings, dismiss our needs, and just keep peddling away on that hamster wheel.

We might even wear our selflessness, our busyness and our lack of regard for our personal wellbeing as a badge of honour. A demonstration, even, of our true courage and commitment to making a difference. 'Oh, it isn't about me!'

The ultimate irony of compassionate practice is that we can lack compassion for ourselves. And the consequences of this are potentially devastating.

THE LOWDOWN ON BURNOUT

The starting point for this book was my own experience, as well as what I learnt and observed as I started talking with others about burnout in recent years. However, in the process of doing the research for this book, even I was alarmed as I dug deep into the prevalence, manifestations and consequences of this problem.

There is a true disconnect between our knowledge and our behaviour – as individuals, in teams, in workplaces and across the sectors as a whole. We have normalised stress, constraint, demands, distress, fatigue and our prevailing culture of busyness.

There are many risk factors, causes and consequences of burnout, which has reached epidemic proportions in the health sector, becoming a fundamental and systemic issue. And that was in normal times prior to the COVID-19 pandemic of 2020. The further toll of the pandemic on our health and social sector workforce is yet to fully emerge but it would be fair to say it hasn't helped!

THE SCALE OF THE PROBLEM
Burnout is reported by around thirty per cent of healthcare workers across Australia, the United States and the United Kingdom, across disciplines and in direct and indirect roles. Rates reported range from seventeen to fifty-two per cent.[4][5][6][7][8][9][10] Job stress and fatigue rates are far higher, and people working in healthcare and social assistance roles are the second highest occupational groupings in relation to claims for mental health conditions.[11]

This is further potentiated by this being our largest industry by employment. Alarmingly, more than one in five doctors in the United States have reported suicidal thoughts, and more than one in 100 have attempted to take their own life. In fact, the rate of suicide among American doctors is double that of the general population.[12][13] In Australia, one in four doctors reported having suicidal thoughts in the past year, and one in fifty reported that they had attempted suicide.[14]

The sustained physical, emotional and psychological demands of our work are literally destroying lives.

This is not sustainable.

We have to reject burnout and choose a different path.

The sustained physical, emotional and psychological demands of our work are literally destroying lives.

CAUTIONARY TALES:

THE MANY MASKS OF BURNOUT

In the following anecdotes about individuals, their colleagues and their workplaces, you can see the many ways in which the pathway of decline – or burnout itself – can manifest.

SUSAN – THE LATE-NIGHT WORKER

Susan works long hours, late into the night, almost every night – and she doesn't miss an opportunity to let her colleagues know it. She has become known for her late-night emails and her audible, exasperated sighs in meetings. She has become a strong contributor to a relentless, pressured, toxic and unsustainable workplace culture. Susan herself is not okay and knows she can't sustain this situation. But she doesn't know how to step out or change the patterns of her work life, or the expectations within the workplace that she has contributed to establishing.

JENNIFER – THE CHANGE RESISTER

Jennifer has been working in a service for many years, and now there's been a change in leadership. She is tired, and she constantly feels the pressure of expectations that the service, currently limited in its reach, needs to expand and grow. Jennifer feels like this is unreasonable and she's not going to have a bar of it. In team and individual discussions, Jennifer is curt and negative. She storms around the workplace and everyone knows she's not happy! Jennifer's behaviour is slowly depleting the energy of every member of her team.

DENISE – THE SELFLESS CRUSADER

Denise proudly wears the badge of honour she has earnt from putting herself last. She readily takes responsibility for the people around her. When Denise sees other people taking care of themselves, she is repelled by this and sees them as selfish. Denise will often take the moral high ground, openly passing judgement on the behaviour and choices of others. Denise doesn't ask for or accept help from others, and, when it's offered, will resist intensely and then complain about the load she carries. Frankly, she drains the energy out of everyone around her.

STEWART – THE TEAMMATE WITH SELECTIVE FOCUS

Stewart is unapologetic in stating that he is not here for the team or the organisation – he is here for the patients. He resists participation in team conversations or activities designed to build connections within the team. Stewart excludes himself from conversations and work related to the overall organisational culture or strategic priorities. When he is not able to opt out, everyone knows he is not happy – and his passive aggressive behaviours and his resistance have a negative effect on his colleagues, diminishing their experience.

KATE – THE BOUNDARY SETTER

Kate feels quite fragile, and has low energy and output – so she knows that she needs to maintain very clear boundaries around work and life in order for her to remain well. Her colleagues believe that working long hours and making personal sacrifices is a sign of a stronger commitment to their work, so they are critical of Kate's approach. Kate experiences this as judgemental and unkind, so she feels disconnected from the team. This further undermines her already low confidence and her sense of contribution.

STEPHANIE – HANDPASSING PRESSURE DOWN THE LINE

Stephanie is absolutely under the pump, and, despite her best efforts, is often faced with the unrealistic expectation of completing major projects within tight deadlines. Stephanie feels completely overwhelmed by her own workload. She works as hard as she can – she has, in fact, never worked so hard in her life. She knows that she can't sustain this and feels herself slipping. She is just so tired and stressed. When meeting with her team, Stephanie is agitated, impatient and demanding. She hasn't got time for small talk, and places pressure on her team to deliver on work that she knows is impossible to complete in such a short period of time. But she doesn't know what else to do.

MARK – THE DISCONNECTED DOCTOR

Mark has worked in health for many years, and he has witnessed the suffering of so many good people. He used to get to know his patients well, and was a much-loved and trusted doctor. In the workplace, despite the challenges he and his team faced, Mark always managed to turn up with a smile and a joke, making the work a little easier and, sometimes, even fun for others. Over a period of many years, Mark has felt a growing heaviness as the toll of long hours and relentless demand has crept up on him. Lately, he has not been his usual self and, to make matters worse, there's been complaints from patients that Mark is blunt in his communication and uncaring. His partner is constantly complaining about the hours he works. Mark finds himself lingering longer at work to avoid having to deal with the kids before bedtime. Mark feels like he is under fire from every direction, and he wonders how he will keep going.

LOUISE – DISTRESSED AND NOT COPING

Louise was being bullied behind closed doors by a member of her team who was struggling with change. Louise was really distressed by this behaviour – and often found herself in tears on the way home and once at home. On the weekends, she would feel lost, and like she just couldn't face her work anymore. Louise asked for help from her boss to deal with the behaviour. While she was given support and a listening ear, Louise was then encouraged to just keep going – to step back into the fray – and told that she was doing a great job. But the daily conflict and tension in the workplace became too much for her to bear. One day, Louise woke up feeling such crippling anxiety and distress that she called her boss to say that she couldn't return to work.

DAVID – THE CYNIC

David feels like he is the main character in *Groundhog Day*. New initiatives, ideas and projects come and go – but it feels like, despite great energy, enthusiasm and effort over the years, that nothing ever changes in a meaningful way. Meanwhile, the fundamental problems that he and his colleagues are facing are never truly addressed. When a new idea or scheme comes along, David digs his heels in, resisting all attempts to engage and participate. What's the point?

Do you recognise any of these masks of burnout in yourself or your colleagues?

CHAPTER 1:

IT'S TIME TO TAKE CONTROL, AND IT STARTS WITH YOU

Bronnie Ware, an Australian author, is well known for her internationally bestselling book, *The Top Five Regrets of the Dying: A life Transformed by the Dearly Departing*.[15] In writing this book, she drew on her experience as a carer for people who were in the final weeks of their life and wished to die in their home. Over time, as part of her carer role, Bronnie started to ask the people she was caring for about 'any regrets they had or anything they would do differently'. Her book centres around this question.

The conversations which resulted were profound, and Bronnie was stunned and moved by the incredible clarity with which people spoke their truth at this time.

A set of common themes emerged from these conversations. As a result, Bronnie penned these in a blog post, 'Regrets of the Dying' – which struck a chord with millions of people who read and shared the post. It was then that Bronnie expanded this story into what would become her internationally bestselling book. The top five regrets were:

- I wish I'd had the courage to live a life true to myself, not the life others expected of me.
- I wish I hadn't worked so much.
- I wish I'd had the courage to express my feelings.
- I wish I had stayed in touch with my friends.
- I wish that I had let myself be happier.

It's important to ask yourself the question: How would you fare across these five dimensions if you were to reflect back on your life so far?

Why is it important to do so?

When you don't take control of and prioritise your wellbeing, you are vulnerable to burnout and may be on a path to regret.

When I look back now on my 'burnout years', these statements resonate strongly with me. I was definitely on a path that would have led to a similar conversation in the final weeks of my own life. If I hadn't changed my course, I would have continued down that path.

BURNOUT AND REGRET

Because burnout is so strongly linked to these kinds of regrets, you need to recognise the many ways you are vulnerable to burnout. Here are some of those ways:

IT'S TIME TO TAKE CONTROL, AND IT STARTS WITH YOU | 35

When your work is purpose-driven, and linked to your personal fulfilment and meaning in life, you are vulnerable.

When you're working within an environment of constant constraint, change, complexity and struggle, you are vulnerable.

When your work creates an environment in which you are directly or indirectly facing trauma, sadness, loss and helplessness, you are vulnerable.

When so many unmet needs and so many competing demands are consuming your time and energy, you are vulnerable.

When you're working with colleagues who are not coping, and whose presence and behaviour drain your energy, you are vulnerable.

When you're finding it hard to see tangible impacts from your work despite great efforts, you are vulnerable.

When you feel that your efforts are unseen, your voice is unheard and your contribution is unvalued, you are vulnerable.

When you simultaneously experience challenges, competing demands and stressors in your personal life, you are vulnerable.

All of these factors will drain your energy and your wellbeing.

It's like this. Imagine a bucket where your energy and wellbeing stores are kept. There are things that top up the reserves in your bucket, and there are holes in your bucket that drain those reserves. Now, if your bucket is draining quicker than it is filling, it's going to empty.

Empty = burnout.

Empty = face down.

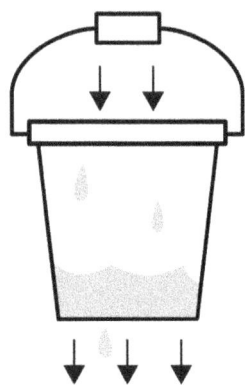

YOU KNOW YOU SHOULD BE TAKING CARE OF YOURSELF – YET OFTEN YOU DON'T

When you work in the health and social sectors, there's always someone who's worse off than you – no matter what you're dealing with personally. You can always find someone with much greater hardship, a more harrowing story, or much greater disadvantages than you have. This disadvantage and suffering and tragedy is front and centre, in your face, all the time. A constant reminder that no matter how bad things get, they could be much worse.

This can lead to unhealthy and unhelpful personal dialogue. Something like this:

IT'S TIME TO TAKE CONTROL, AND IT STARTS WITH YOU | 37

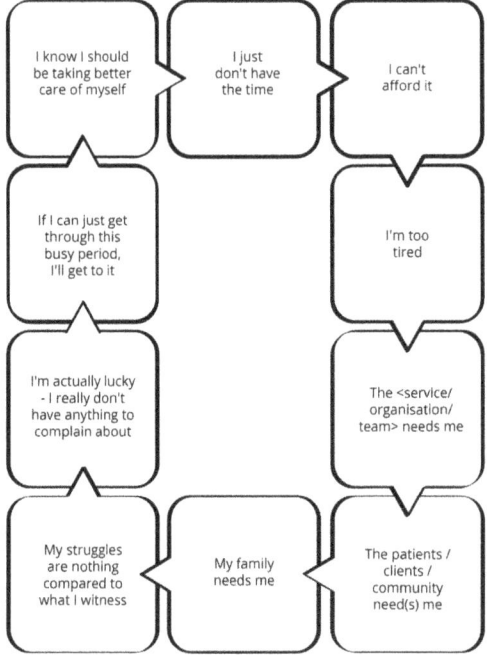

This internal dialogue is what propels you to 'just keep going' and to feel like you don't have the luxury of stopping. You cue that hamster wheel, step on it and just keep peddling.

These thoughts and actions are all derived from pure intentions. To turn up in service to others. To make a difference through your work. To be there for your family. They can be linked to your inherent sense of self-worth and aligned with your fundamental values. But they can also contribute to your path to burnout – because, in all of these internal dialogue steps, you are not focusing on yourself. Your individual needs are not a priority. Your wellbeing is not in focus. You don't matter as much as everyone and everything else.

You have to shift these patterns and change this dialogue because

While compassion for others is a cornerstone of the philosophy of the health and social sectors, and probably the reason why you get out of bed to go to work each morning, this is not what is going to sustain you.

you otherwise risk working yourself into a stupor. Literally! This isn't good for you, your family, your life – and certainly not good for your work and your sector. While compassion for others is a cornerstone of the philosophy of the health and social sectors, and probably the reason why you get out of bed to go to work each morning, this is not what is going to sustain you.

ARE YOU ON A PATH TO REGRET?

Unless you are finding ways to rest, and to restore and replenish your reserves, your bucket is going to empty. And somewhere along the way, you might find that you are on a path towards one or more of those five regrets. Take a look at the following examples to see how common mistakes made by those working in the health and social sectors could eventually lead to those five regrets.

You may have dispensed with long-held personal dreams because it just feels too hard to pursue them.

> *I wish I'd had the courage to live a life true to myself, not the life others expected of me.*

You work harder and longer hours.

> *I wish I hadn't worked so much.*

You close down and don't ask for help or share how you are feeling.

> *I wish I'd had the courage to express my feelings.*

You spend less time with friends and extended family because you're always so busy – and, when you do have downtime, you just don't have the energy to socialise.

I wish I had stayed in touch with my friends.

You lose focus of the things that make you happy, your own nurturing doesn't even make it onto the list, and you consistently put yourself and your needs last.

I wish that I had let myself be happier.

PUTTING YOURSELF FIRST IS THE ONLY ANSWER

I learnt the hardest of ways – when I was face down and didn't know whether or how I would recover – that putting myself first was in fact the only answer.

You matter, the work you do matters, and your life matters too. If you don't put yourself first and take great care of you, who's going to?

The primary responsibility for you starts and ends with you, and you need to take control.

You can't pour from an empty cup.

THE RELATIONSHIP BETWEEN COMPASSION FOR OURSELVES AND FOR OTHERS

Let's explore the relationship between compassion for ourselves and for others.

The primary responsibility for you starts and ends with you, and you need to take control.

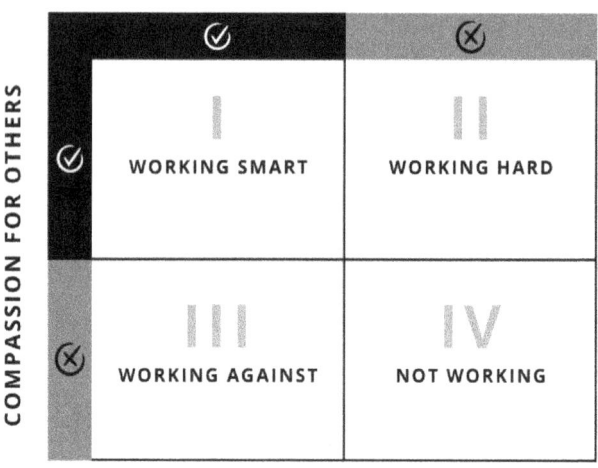

Let's take a closer look at each part of this compassion model.

QUADRANT I: WORKING SMART

In Quadrant I, you have self-compassion and compassion for others. This is optimal. I would also argue that compassion for yourself needs to come first, because this is where the magic happens. When you operate in this quadrant, you have an optimal capacity that allows you to make and sustain impact through your work, ensuring that it is not at the expense of other things that you hold dear.

When you are working in this quadrant, you have clarity, you feel aligned with your purpose and things just feel a little easier, like they flow freely rather than being a constant struggle. You will derive a greater sense of fulfilment from your work as you won't be weighed down by the sacrifices you have made or the continual feeling that you are compromised. You are pressure-proof – you have the capacity to remain resilient in the face of challenges and dramas, and you will be an inspiration to and a positive role model for others.

QUADRANT II: WORKING HARD

In Quadrant II, others come first. You have compassion for others but not for yourself. This is the quadrant that you might feel the most comfortable in and that appeals to the selfless, self-sacrificing, 'It's not about me' philosophy. You can also be in this quadrant for a long time and achieve some great things. But can you go the distance? I would argue that a lack of compassion for myself is what perpetuated my decline to burnout and it could do for you, too. This is where burnout may feel or be inevitable, depending on the circumstances of your work and life. Being in this quadrant is not optimal – nor is it sustainable.

When you are working in this quadrant, you may be achieving a lot and creating impact, but it feels like a hard slog. You are vulnerable, and you risk hitting the deck when a crisis occurs in work or life (or both). While people may admire you, you set an unhealthy and unhelpful benchmark for your team and organisation, which actually means you are not a great role model for others.

QUADRANT III: WORKING AGAINST

In Quadrant III, you are compassionate towards yourself but not towards others. This is not optimal and, if sustained, could come at a significant cost to the culture and productivity of your organisation and team. Your own contribution won't be optimal as you are unlikely to be as connected to the organisation's mission as others, and this may result in criticism, conflict and strained workplace relationships. You are not a team player, and you contribute to frustration and resentment within your workplace, especially for those who are operating in Quadrant II. You may actively resist change or growth and create barriers to progress. These workplace challenges will be a drain on the team.

QUADRANT IV: NOT WORKING

Quadrant IV is not a happy place to be. This is where you do not have compassion for yourself or for others. This is toxic for everyone. You will be a drain on the energy and wellbeing of others with your cynicism and – perhaps – with your difficult or destructive behaviour. You may blame and resent others, and you are not likely to take responsibility for yourself, your role, and the impact you have on others. This will divert precious resources into dealing with your inappropriate behaviour and its negative impacts on your team and work culture.

THE IMPORTANCE OF CHOOSING QUADRANT I AND PUTTING YOURSELF FIRST

After looking at these quadrants, it becomes clear that the most powerful thing you can do in order to be of service to others is, in fact, to put yourself first.

A lack of self-compassion limits your capacity to sustain your efforts.

It limits the impact you make and, as a result, also limits the connection between your work and your sense of purpose and meaning.

It affects the lives and work of others in a negative way.

The most powerful thing you can do in order to be of service to others is, in fact, to put yourself first.

It ensures you become part of the problem, not the solution.

It's time to change that. Here's how.

EXERCISE: FIND YOUR STARTING POINT

Reflect on where you sit in this compassion model at the moment. Then, answer these questions:

- Do you need to dial up your focus on you?
- What do you stand to gain by putting yourself first, with compassion for yourself (first) *and* compassion for others (second)?
- What do you stand to lose if you don't put yourself first?

Then, consider the dimensions covered in the following questions, by answering them too:

- Do you feel a sense of control over your life and your work?
- Are you making positive, healthful choices that serve you well?
- Are you happy with the impact that you are making?
- Are your energy levels high, or is your bucket running low?
- Do you feel like you are on a sustainable or unsustainable path at the moment?

BURNOUT FACTS #2:

HOW BURNOUT MANIFESTS AND WHY IT MATTERS

Burnout is an insidious problem that is commonly described as a condition that can slowly creep up on you. It can manifest after a long, slow decline and be well advanced by the time you are even paying attention to it. You might not recognise the signs and symptoms, and it may endure for a very long time before you sense any danger, let alone feel emboldened to act. Often, it is when you are face down, well after much damage has been done, that action is taken as a matter of necessity rather than as a proactive choice.

Burnout is a direct consequence of chronic workplace stress that has not been successfully managed – and, in the health and social sectors, chronic stress is the rule, not the exception. Unhealthy social and cultural norms work against meaningful efforts to prevent or reduce stress. Demand for our services, and unmet health and social needs, are growing. Healthcare practice is becoming increasingly complex – and the many, often competing, demands on our time and energy, coupled with relentless resource constraints, are simply and devastatingly wearing us down.

Burnout is commonly characterised by three dimensions:

1. **Emotional exhaustion:** The depletion of emotional, physical and mental energy, leaving a person drained and fatigued

2. **Depersonalisation:** A withdrawal or distancing from one's

work that might manifest as a level of detachment, callousness, indifference or negativity. This can be associated with a loss of empathy, and a sense of apathy and cynicism.

3. Reduced personal efficacy: A loss of confidence in our competence and sense of accomplishment; a feeling of ineptitude that may further precipitate a loss of drive or sense of care about achieving, leading to decreased function and reduced effectiveness.[16]

BURNOUT CAN FEEL LIKE...

- Stress, pressure
- Loss of confidence
- Feeling inadequate, self-critical, guilty
- Powerlessness, demoralisation, a lack of value
- Disconnection from meaning, satisfaction, joy and passion that you once derived from work
- Being trapped, lacking motivation and fulfilment
- Dissatisfaction with work and life
- Dread, intrusive thoughts, mood swings
- Numbness
- Isolation, alienation
- Confusion, a lack of mental clarity
- Anxiety, distress, overwhelm
- A relentless struggle, restlessness

BEHAVIOURS ASSOCIATED WITH BURNOUT

A range of behaviours associated with burnout, which can actually further precipitate decline, include:

- Social and psychological withdrawal, such as reduced empathy, compassion and a sense of joy or humour
- Avoidance, such as an aversion to going to work, avoiding contact with workmates, or a lack of will to work
- Numbing, such as the drink after work, craving comfort food, or other vices as a replacement for energy and health
- Difficulty concentrating, such as challenges in performing normal activities, difficulty prioritising, difficulty keeping track of simple information, easily distracted, forgetful, error-prone
- Lack of emotional regulation – trouble keeping calm, highly emotionally reactive, growing irritability, tired and cranky, impatient, snappy with staff
- Lack of healthy boundaries, such as going to heroic lengths to survive a work environment that's brimming with barriers and frustrations [17][18][19][20][21][22]

WHY DOES BURNOUT MATTER?

For the person going through it, the psychological and physical consequences of burnout are significant. They can range from insomnia and other sleep disturbances to a range of physical manifestations that can mimic serious illness. Burnout impairs our capacity to sustain our professional work, with many contemplating leaving their workplace or even their profession. The spillover effect into our personal life can be significant, and lead to strains and conflicts in personal relationships, relationship breakdowns, and worse.

In our workplaces, burnout can impact negatively on our colleagues, have damaging flow-on effects on the health workforce, and have a negative influence on workplace culture and functioning. Toxic behaviours and workplace cultures can precipitate, and the growing impact of staff absenteeism and turnover can take a heavy toll on the system. This further compromises the quality and continuity of care, adding significant resource burdens to an already over-stretched system.

The experiences of our patients, carers and communities – those who we are here to serve directly and indirectly – are also affected. Burnout compromises patient or client experiences, and impacts on the quality and safety of care. Ultimately, this can negatively influence outcomes, working in contrast to the very reason that we chose to do the work we do.

A CAUTIONARY TALE:

ON A PATH TOWARDS BURNOUT

Here's what happens when you don't put yourself first.

Sylvia has had some remarkable opportunities in her career so far, and she feels like she has fought and worked very hard for each and every one of them. She has been a vocal advocate for the rights and unmet needs of a relatively small group with extraordinarily complex needs and poor health outcomes. A group that had fallen through the gaps and were not being seen or heard in our busy health system. Her advocacy efforts have influenced policy, practice and funding, and there are now more services available and a greater investment in research to truly seek to improve outcomes.

Sylvia's efforts have not gone unrecognised. She is seen as a leader in her country and also internationally in her field. Despite the achievements and gains over time, and clear recognition of need for this group, it remains a constant battle to maintain service provision. Funding is cobbled together from multiple sources and is never quite enough to provide all of the services that this patient group needs. Attracting and retaining a high-performing team is a real challenge, as there isn't enough funding available to compete with the salaries and conditions offered elsewhere. The different funding sources all come with unique reporting requirements. There are times when Sylvia feels like all she ever does is compile data and write reports. When not doing this, she is fighting to retain existing funding and writing submissions to seek additional funding support.

Sylvia feels like her current working life is a million miles away from when she was working directly with patients early in her career. She finds the daily struggle of fighting to retain core services incredibly frustrating, and it feels like so much time, energy and expertise are being wasted in just maintaining the status quo. And then, a staff member resigns, and Sylvia's efforts are diverted to recruitment. It feels, at times, like all she ever does is put out fires. Meanwhile, there are needs that are not met and further reach that could be achieved but that feels impossible with such limited capacity. The entire situation is completely and utterly exhausting.

Sylvia has always had a very strong work ethic. She works hard and long hours, and she is dedicated to the cause she has championed for all of these years. She is also proud of what she has achieved. Unfortunately, many people have died along the way, and Sylvia feels a deep sense of sadness whenever she reflects on particular patients with whom she had a strong connection. The pall of sadness feels a little heavier each time another person dies.

With daily frustrations and challenges as present as ever, Sylvia wonders just how much longer she can sustain things as they are. She's unsure of what the next step for her could be. Opportunities are limited, her energy levels are low, and she finds herself feeling unvalued, unheard, and resentful of others who seem to have a better deal. It feels like the scales have tipped in such a way that the personal sacrifices Sylvia has made and what she has gained from them are out of balance.

I am sure Sylvia's story resonates with many. Sylvia's hard work and passionate commitment is admirable, and she has clearly operated from Quadrant II of the compassion model, working hard, for many

years, putting the needs of others before her own. Making sacrifices to stay the course and fight the good fight to retain the focus and funding for these important services. Working hard, achieving great things but, all the while, on a path towards burnout.

LOOKING AHEAD

In Part 2, you will explore and face the current truth of your work *and* life. By working through a series of steps, you will start to see an alternative pathway emerging and be inspired to believe that work *and* life don't have to feel so hard. You will also be inspired to believe that the joy, challenge and meaning that you once derived or anticipated getting from your work can actually become a reality and add value to the whole of your life.

We will look at a range of ways you can shift your mindset, liberate your energy, and improve your focus one tiny step at a time. We will also look at how to create your very own personal impact plan that drives meaningful progress.

By reviewing these elements, you will learn how to put yourself first most effectively. This matters, because, contrary to our anecdotes of heroic selfless feats, putting yourself first could be the most responsible and courageous thing you could ever do. In doing this, you could increase the impact you make in the world – not lessen it.

PART 2

GETTING PRACTICAL AND ZOOMING IN ON YOU

The problem of burnout is clear, and if this is or has been a part of your experience, you can rest assured that you are not alone. Perhaps you've felt a sinking feeling as you've read the book so far, reflecting on your own situation. Perhaps you've recognised burnout in yourself, either in the present or the past, or maybe you feel at risk of burnout if you don't make some changes. Hopefully, as you've been reading, you've considered what putting yourself first might look like or where you would even start. This might feel liberating to you – or you might feel anxious and uneasy.

Never fear!

In Part 2, we'll get super practical, and I will take you, step by gentle step, through a process of creating a rock-solid plan that gets you from where you are now to where you need and deserve to be.

You will do this through developing INSIGHT, creating an enabling MINDSET, and building your ENERGY reserves.

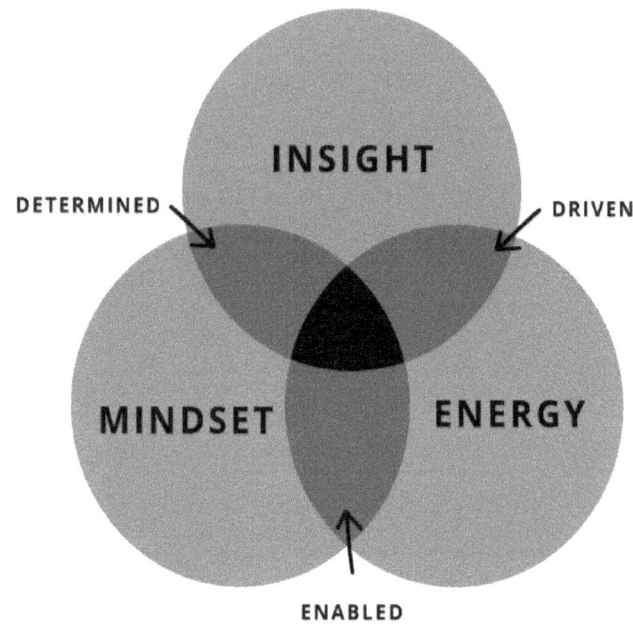

When these three elements come together, you know what you need to do, you have the **determination** and **drive** to do it, and you will have **enabled** your capacity to reject burnout and blaze a trail instead.

In Chapter 2, we'll focus on developing INSIGHT. You will do this by facing the truth of your situation, exploring what matters to you, and identifying some key areas that you need to focus on as a starting point as you reclaim yourself, your time, your wellbeing, and your full capacity to make a difference.

In Chapter 3, we'll look at the ways you can create an enabling MINDSET. This will help you stay on track, remain focused, optimise the energy you have available, and help you move in the right direction now and in the future.

In Chapter 4, we'll identify the ways you can build your ENERGY reserves. Doing this is the most critical enabler of your sustained and meaningful progress.

Working step by step through the activities in Part 2, you will create the basis for your very own personal impact plan – a plan that will put you on the path to your best work *and* your best life.

Let's get started.

CHAPTER 2

INSIGHT: FACE YOUR TRUTH

Insight: the ability to have a clear, deep and sometimes sudden understanding of a complicated problem or situation.[23]

In the movie *National Treasure*, Nicholas Cage's character and his fellow treasure hunters work their way through a series of encrypted clues, adventures and perils in their search for ancient hidden treasures that are worth billions of dollars.

To solve one of the clues, the hero of the story uses a pair of glasses with different-coloured lenses, which he adjusts to reveal hidden messages on a seemingly blank piece of paper.

I have often found myself thinking of this movie scene and of the concept of the combination of different-coloured lenses that create different-coloured filters through which we look.

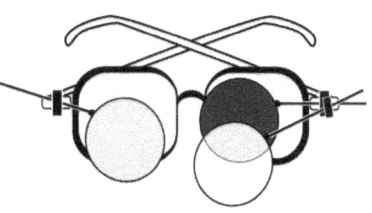

Imagine these glasses, but with an infinite number of coloured lenses and combinations of those colours. Then imagine that the lenses you use and their colours are determined by your unique self, your personality, and the circumstances and experiences of your life. Imagine, too, that these lenses and colours may change over time, based on your experiences and the lessons learnt along the way.

Looking through your set of lenses, you have an absolutely unique perspective on the world. What you see, hear and feel, and what you make those things mean, is guided by your internal narrative.

It is how you process and make sense of the world, and of your place in it.

STOP, REFLECT AND TAKE STOCK

I wonder when you last took some time out of your busy life to reflect on what truly matters to you. The things that light you up, make you happy, and that bring satisfaction, fulfilment and meaning to your life. To explore how you're feeling and track your progress – what's working, what's not working and what needs to change?

In the busy environment of your life, perhaps while you are peddling away on that hamster wheel, you might not even think about yourself at all. Or you might not want to go there for fear of what it will bring up. It's possible you've even just surrendered to your 'lot in life'. It might look a bit like this:

Looking through your set of lenses, you have an absolutely unique perspective on the world. What you see, hear and feel, and what you make those things mean, is guided by your internal narrative.

It is how you process and make sense of the world, and of your place in it.

The relentlessly busy environment.

There's never enough time, energy, resources ... or enough of you to go around.

The normalised misery of your workplace or of other aspects of your life.

The challenging interactions with colleagues and others.

The toxic culture and behaviours that have become the norm.

When it comes to all of these, it could even be reasonable to conclude that you have no power to influence them. These features of your life appear simply out of your control.

However, they *are* in your control. You can make your 'lot in life' better. If you want to step forward in a way that is aligned with you, your goals, your values and what matters to you, you have to start by reflecting and creating insight. Just like you would collect data, consult with key stakeholders, or do an environmental scan when considering a new initiative in your work.

You may be thinking, 'I don't have time.' But that isn't true. You can choose to make time and I would argue strongly that you can't afford not to.

There is no more perfect time to stop and take stock than this moment right here and now. It is the very first step towards you regaining control over yourself and your life.

In this chapter, you will take a good, hard look through your set of lenses – and be guided to develop insight into your unique, wonderful self. You will explore the meaning of work in the context of your life, what matters to you in your work and in your life, and the current status of your bucket – your energy and wellbeing reserves, the in-flows and the out-flows.

Step by step, these insights will come together to create a picture of you now. You will identify the areas of yourself and your life that need attention, your pain points, and the things that matter to you that are suffering from neglect. You will also identify the potential areas for focus where the greatest gains can be made for the least effort. This is an important part of the process, because the last thing you want is to be overwhelmed. There's enough of that already in your life.

Let's get started!

UNDERSTANDING HOW WORK AND LIFE INTERSECT FOR YOU

We'll start the process of creating insight by considering the place of work within the context of your life. To do this, we'll first look at some of the thoughts explored by Chris Helder in his book, *Useful Belief*. In this book, Helder makes a series of observations about the separation of our personal and professional lives as they exist across multiple generations.[24]

For **Baby Boomers**, Helder describes a division between work and life. Work was something that was done within particular hours to earn a living, and life consisted of everything else. As a result, the two were quite separate.

When looking at **Generation X**, he describes this as the first generation in which there is an overlap between work and life. This is often termed 'the generation that could have it all'! Work influences life, and life influences work.

Finally, Helder describes **Generation Y** as having a complete overlap between work and life. This generation is hyper-connected, always on, and lacking boundaries between work and the rest of their lives. Just a single concept all mixed in together.

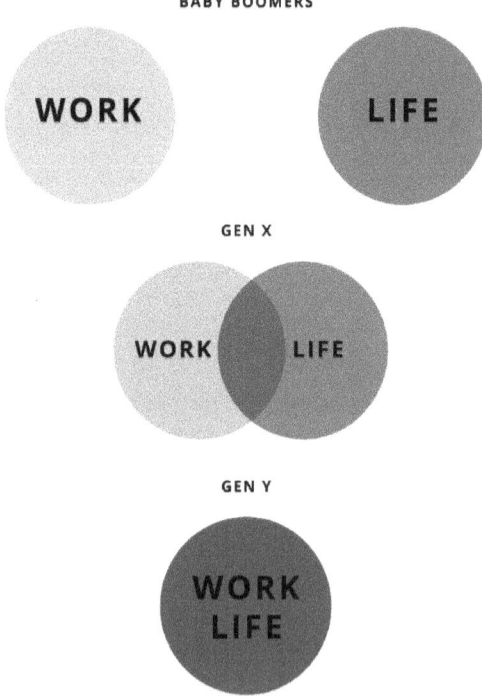

There are cultural and societal constructs reflected in Helder's description of work and life across the generations, which means there are assumptions in his book that won't universally apply. However, his conception of these generations' work-life balance is useful, as it warrants consideration in the process of developing insight here.

Overlaid on these generational differences is your personal vocation in pursuing a career in the health and/or social sector. If your fundamental motivation for work is to make a difference in the lives of others, your work will be intrinsically linked to your sense of purpose – so it will, as a result, influence the meaning and fulfilment you derive from your life overall. Your work-life circles might overlap a lot, a little or entirely.

Where there is overlap, you will find work spilling over into the rest of your life in both positive and negative ways. Your personal life will also have a positive and negative influence on your work.

To develop insight into how this occurs within your own life, work through the following exercise.

EXERCISE: UNDERSTAND YOUR WORK-LIFE OVERLAP

To complete this exercise, you'll want to consider these questions and your answers to them:

1. What do your circles look like? Consider the impact of your generation and also the role that your work has in terms of your sense of purpose.

2. Are they separate or do they overlap? If they overlap, by how much?
3. What does the degree of this overlap mean for you? How does your personal life influence your work, and how does your work influence your personal life?
4. Thinking about where you are at now (consider the last month), what are the positive and negative influences of your work on your life? What are the positive and negative influences of your life on your work?

HOW BUMPY IS YOUR RIDE ON THE WHEEL OF LIFE NOW?

Understanding your wheel of life is another way to gain the insight you need.

This concept of the 'Wheel of Life' is considered to have first been developed in the 1960s by Paul Meyer. It has since been adapted into a diagnostic tool that people use to create a simple snapshot of what matters to them most in life and how satisfied they are with their current situation. Since its conception and adaptation, the wheel of life has been widely adopted.

In the following exercise, we'll step through the process of creating your unique wheel of life.

EXERCISE: WHEEL OF LIFE

1. Start by doing a brainstorm of all of the things that are important to you in life, jotting them down as you go. Don't worry about how many concepts you come up with. Here are a few options to get your thinking started (that are not intended to limit you in any way): children, partner, friendships, family, physical health, career, money, fun, growth, spirituality, social life, wellbeing, mental health, exercise, recreation, adventure, travel, leisure time, learning, creativity, joy, making a difference, hobbies, freedom, choice, and music.
2. Reflect on your initial list, and use the following questions to help you focus in on the dimensions that are critically important to you: What matters to you most in your life? What lights you up? What do you need? Circle those.
3. Are there some common themes that are emerging? If so, can you narrow these themes down to the eight things that matter to you most? When you look at the refined list, does it feel like anything that is critically important to you is missing? Keep refining it until you are certain that all the things that matter are included.
4. Now that you have your list of eight dimensions, write the name of each dimension in each outermost section of the wheel that follows.

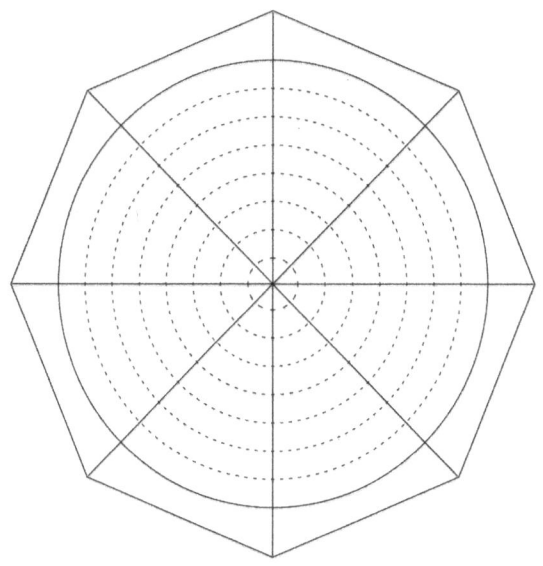

5. It's time now to rate your level of satisfaction for each dimension, from '0: Completely unsatisfied' (the centre of the wheel) to '8: Very satisfied' (the outer edge of the wheel). You are rating your level of satisfaction in this current moment in time. It is not a picture of how life has been in the past, nor is it what you might like it to be in the future. It is a current snapshot of your life now - warts and all.

I've provided an example here so you can see what I mean.

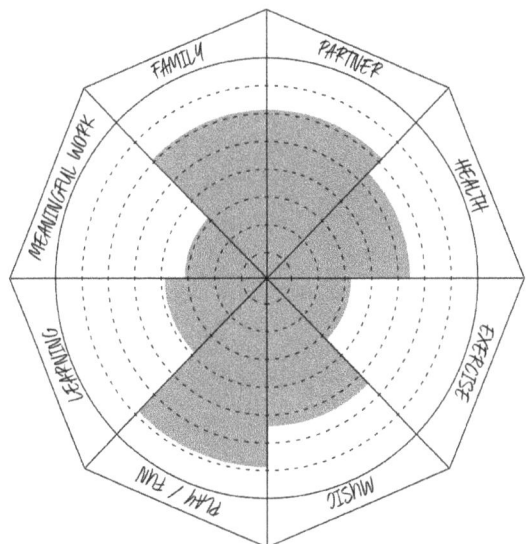

6. Take a look at what the outer perimeter of your wheel of life looks like based on the ratings you have given each segment of your wheel. Trace that line with your finger or pen and consider the answers to these questions:

- If this were a wheel on a bicycle, how bumpy would my ride be?
- What am I neglecting?
- Where's the pain?
- In what areas do I need to increase my levels of satisfaction?
- Where would I focus my efforts to get the greatest return?

HOW FULL IS YOUR BUCKET?

The final step in creating insight is to consider the status of your energy and wellbeing bucket.

Many years ago, I read a book called *How Full Is Your Bucket?* This book, penned by grandson and grandfather Tom Rath and Don Clifton, is about the very simple metaphor of a bucket with a dipper. The bucket represents your stores of positive emotions, and the dipper representing interactions and experiences with others where they either take from or add to your bucket.

> 'We are at our best when our buckets are overflowing and at our worst when they are empty.'[25]

A number of years ago, I was introduced to a similar concept used by specialist counsellor Liz Crocker: the 'living well'. She explores this concept in her recently published book, *The Patient Advocate Handbook*.[26] This 'living well' represents the finite energy resources you have available to allocate to all the areas of your life. Liz argues that each person has a finite amount of energy that they can allocate. When we are overloaded and our energy stores become depleted, we can end up running on adrenaline. Liz describes the inevitable 'crash' that occurs when the adrenaline eventually runs out.

In the past few years, I've drawn on these metaphors to create a mechanism to assess your current status, and to assist you in taking control and improving your wellbeing. Think about a bucket as your stores of energy and wellbeing. There are things that fill your bucket – they give you energy, make you feel positive, and add value to your life. There are things that drain your bucket – they sap your energy and vitality, and leave you feeling depleted.

You can't avoid drains on your energy – having to do things that you don't like doing, having difficult conversations, dealing with conflict, loss, grief and life challenges...

But here's the thing: if your bucket is draining quicker than it is filling, it is going to empty.

Here's what your bucket might look like, and what you should do depending on what it looks like.

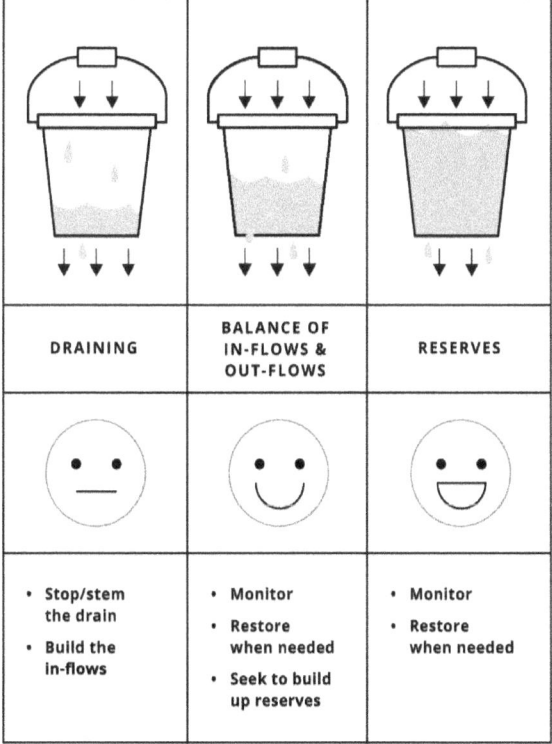

If your bucket is draining quicker than it is filling, it is going to empty.

If your bucket is **draining**, you need to: 1) Stop/stem the drain, and 2) Build the in-flow.

If you have a **balance of in-flows and out-flows**, it is important to: 1) Monitor how you're going so you can notice early if you are out of balance and at risk of draining, 2) Restore when needed, and 3) Seek to build up reserves to provide a buffer for the challenges that are yet to come.

If you have ample **reserves**, I suspect you are not actually reading this book! If you do, well done, and keep doing what you're doing. Monitor how you're going once more so you can identify any risks to your reserves decreasing and restore when needed.

Now let's focus on your current bucket, by completing an exercise.

EXERCISE: HOW FULL IS YOUR BUCKET?

1. Draw a simple bucket.
2. Add the water level that reflects the level of energy and wellbeing you feel you have and are experiencing now – and that represents how you've felt about these over the course of the past month or two.
3. Think about your in-flows and out-flows. Are they about even? Is there more coming in than going out, or do you feel like your bucket is draining? Add arrows above and below your bucket to

represent the amount of in-flows and out-flows you are currently experiencing.
4. What category does your bucket fall into? 'Draining', 'Balance of in-flows and out-flows', or 'Reserves'?
5. Now, turn your attention to the ways you might stop the drain and build the in-flows to your bucket.

5a. If you want to stop or stem the drain, you first need to identify what your unique bucket drainers are. Identify the specific drainers that are impacting on your energy and wellbeing. Some of these will be within your control, and others will be outside of it, due to the circumstances of your life or to the influences or behaviours of others. Include them all.

The following list works as a starting point for you to reflect on (again, this is not designed to limit your thinking).

- Accident
- Anxiety
- A workload that exceeds your available time and energy or that doesn't give you room to breathe
- Being busy
- Carer responsibilities
- Challenging or distressing emotions experienced by people you care about
- Change
- Competing demands and priorities

- Conflict
- Constrained resources
- Decision-making
- Distress
- Emotional situations
- Extended family needs
- Feeling unseen, unheard or unvalued
- Grief and loss
- Guilt
- Illness, physical and/or mental (afflicting you or someone you care for)
- Intimate partner relationship
- Loneliness or isolation
- Money worries
- Moving house
- Negative aspects of your living situation
- Parenting challenges
- Responsibility that feels like a heavy burden
- Risks
- Self-esteem and self-worth issues
- Shame
- Stress
- Time challenges, such as feeling like there aren't enough hours in the day
- 'Toxic' behaviours of others, such as negativity, aggression, manipulation, being demeaning, and being judgemental
- Transitions in life and work

5b. Reflecting on your drainers, consider where there are opportunities for you to reduce the drain by answering the following questions:

- Which drainers can I avoid, reduce or remove – and how?
- Which of the drainers are worsened by the meaning I give to them or how I respond to them? Could I choose to respond differently, and, if so, would that give me some relief?

5c. Now, for the fun part, it's time to identify what fills your bucket. These are the things that light you up, make you smile, give you joy, make you feel energised, and contribute to your wellbeing. Again, here's a list to get your thinking started in developing your own list. I encourage you to get as specific as you can.

- Being creative
- Being in nature
- Belonging
- Connection
- Dancing
- Deep breathing
- Exercising
- Feeling heard, acknowledged and valued
- Financial security
- Gardening
- Going on a holiday

- Gratitude
- Having fun
- Kindness from others
- Kindness to yourself
- Laughter
- Listening to music
- Love
- Meditation
- Mindfulness
- Pampering yourself
- Quiet time
- Reading
- Rest
- Setting boundaries
- Sewing
- Singing
- Sleep
- Spending time with people you care about
- Sunshine
- Taking a day off
- When others support you or offer help

5d. Consider your list, and think about possible simple changes you could make in your life or to your routines to increase those in-flows.

5e. To make these changes, consider the answer to this question: What needs to change to get you to a state of balance or, better still, to where you have reserves?

Being in a place where your energy and wellbeing is in balance, or you have reserves to spare, is what will enable you to withstand the challenges that life will inevitably bring, helping to prevent you from ending up face down.

Ultimately, being in a place where your energy and wellbeing is in balance, or you have reserves to spare, is what will enable you to withstand the challenges that life will inevitably bring, helping to prevent you from ending up face down.

YOU KNOW WHAT YOU NEED TO DO

Too often, we don't even take a moment to stop, breathe, and reflect on how we're feeling and where we are at. We can even lose sight of the things that truly matter to us as we get caught up on that hamster wheel.

But now, you have a way to change that.

By completing the reflective exercises in this chapter, you have invested in creating much-needed insight. You might even feel a little less burdened because of the clarity you have created regarding what matters to you, how you are faring at the moment, and being consciously aware of your fillers, drainers and areas that you choose to work on.

What you may have been feeling in your gut or may have been avoiding is now clear to you – or is at least starting to come into focus. And, as can be the case with this kind of clarity, there may be a series of difficult emotions and feelings that have subsided or alternatively have risen up: overwhelm, fear, helplessness, a sense that things are outside of your control, or that it's all too hard. Aaaargh!

So, take a breath, and don't feel like you have to know what the next steps are at this point. Then, work your way to Chapter 4, where we'll explore ways you can create an enabling MINDSET.

Keep this Elizabeth Gilbert quotation in mind as you do:

> 'Do whatever brings you to life, then. Follow your own fascinations, obsessions and compulsions. Trust them. Create whatever causes a revolution in your heart.'[27]

BURNOUT FACTS #3

WHY WE'RE BURNING OUT IN THE HEALTH AND SOCIAL SECTORS

Despite being characterised in 1974, it took another forty-five years for burnout to be formally recognised in the International Classification of Diseases as an occupational phenomenon resulting from chronic workplace stress that has not been successfully managed.[28] The risk of burnout is influenced by factors at five different levels: society, the system, the workplace, the work role, and individual factors.

Let's explore the first levels of society and the system here.

BURNOUT AS AN ISSUE OF MODERN SOCIETY

The extraordinary technology that enables so much freedom and functionality in our lives and work can also keep us hyper-connected, busy, occupied, online, and available to others twenty-four hours a day, seven days a week.

A culture of 'busyness' has become the norm with the increasing pressure that we impose on ourselves or that is externally imposed on us to work harder and longer. This means working not only longer hours in each day, but also more years in total in our working lives.

When our work is in the health and social sectors, there can be external social pressure imposed on us to stay the course of doing our 'good work'. At times, I felt a heavy burden to stay on that hamster wheel when I knew I was not okay and suspected it was not something I could sustain. Through our work, we have the potential to change the experience and outcomes of people in need, and, at times, to literally save lives. Of course, many of the problems we face are not simply or quickly fixed – and we need to sustain our efforts for years to make a meaningful difference. I vividly remember a colleague who used to say regularly, 'I know I'm demanding, but I've faced this thing and women are dying. We have no time to lose.' This sense of pressure and urgency that we impose on ourselves and others can weigh us down and run counter to our best efforts.

PREVAILING NORMS IN A SYSTEM THAT'S SIMPLY NOT GOOD FOR OUR HEALTH

Despite shifts in our national conversations and in perspectives on mental health, the stigma still abounds, even in the health sector itself! Norms of strength and stoicism prevail, and despite the statistics that show that burnout is inherent in our sector, we feel stigmatised if we demonstrate weakness, show vulnerabilities or ask for help.

Stunningly, a survey of over 15,000 US doctors showed that almost twenty per cent of respondents had considered or accessed 'secret mental healthcare'.[29] [30] This included travelling for more than an hour to a provider, using a different name, and not claiming through insurance so their help-seeking wouldn't be discovered. In Australia, around forty per cent of doctors considered that health professionals with a history of mental health disorders were perceived as less competent than their peers, with an alarming fifty-nine per cent considering being a mental health patient an embarrassment.[31]

While guidelines for managing mental health in the workplace are being developed at a global level, we have yet to see action at a systems level. This would occur through policy and guidelines that drive the acknowledgement and management of burnout as a serious occupational health and safety risk in the health system.

Added to these prevailing norms, there are many system-level pressures that influence our capacity to survive, let alone thrive, in the health and social sectors. Our system is characterised by growing demand and the complexity of need and practice. Change is the norm, resources are chronically strained, and continued striving is the only way to make meaningful progress. Let's explore a few of these inherent pressures further.

The models that are used to determine funding allocations for health services are often based on activity levels – and there is a challenge in keeping pace with contemporary practice or models of care. As a result, we may fall short of the resources that we need to provide evidence-based, best-practice care, despite this being a standard and minimum expectation. Funding constraints and budget cuts place further pressure on the fundamental raw materials in the sector: our people.

Additional funding is often available from governments or other sources such as philanthropic organisations. While these are important contributions, they are often provided in small one-off grants that come with many strings attached. The reliance on this funding, sometimes for core service provision, brings added challenges and pressures on workloads as we continually search and apply for funding.

Even when successful in securing additional funding, we can feel like a slave to many masters – with a burdensome level of reporting requirements adding to the existing pressure within our roles.

Funders expect their investments to go as far as possible and to be leveraged. While funding may be provided to enable the development or testing of a new technique or model of care, there is often the expectation that, if shown to be effective, the new initiative will be implemented on a sustainable basis and without further funding support.

Short-term, one-off funding also creates an additional set of pressures as we seek to attract and retain talented people in our teams. We may not be in a position to offer permanent employment, and good people move from contract to contract, lacking job security and continuity of employment. At an organisational level, this brings challenges, when we have personnel who often move on before a project is complete as they seek greater job security. This places further challenges on our capacity to deliver on the funding requirements and meet funder expectations.

At a professional level, there are certification, education and registration requirements to fulfil to maintain competency to practise in clinical roles. There are expectations that clinicians will demonstrate leadership through making active contributions to the wider field, either in their specific specialty area or more broadly. This may be through presenting at conferences, publishing in the peer-reviewed literature, participating in the education of students and graduates, undertaking research, and participating in quality improvement and project work. At a service, jurisdictional and national level, we are called on to join committees and working groups to participate in wider sector-level reforms.

These pressures are endemic throughout the system.

> Do more with less.
> Work smarter, not harder (without additional time, resources or space for thinking).
> Reduce costs.
> Eliminate waste.
> Innovate.
> Leverage.
> Transform.

And you were already feeling exhausted and weighed down before reading that list, right?

These system-level pressures add to the heavy burdens we carry. They add time and workload pressure, and they compound our fatigue in all its guises: project fatigue, change fatigue, and simple bone-weary tiredness.

These system-level pressures add to the heavy burdens we carry. They add time and workload pressure, and they compound our fatigue in all its guises: project fatigue, change fatigue, and simple bone-weary tiredness.

A CAUTIONARY TALE

FROM INSPIRING TO FACE DOWN

Here's what happens when you don't face your truth.

Lesley was the founding manager of a health service. She'd seen many services that were started with great intentions but that often fell short of these intentions in implementation. Lesley was determined that this one would be different.

From the earliest days, it was clear that there would be challenges. It seemed that no matter what was achieved, there were always unmet needs – people who could not or did not access the service, or things that could be done better.

There were multiple and often competing interests and needs at play. There were never enough resources to scale the service to meet the needs of the people it was designed to serve. At times, Lesley felt like she was constantly going into battle to resist pressure for growth without adequate resources and thus avoid compromising the quality of the service.

Lesley put her heart and soul into her work. There were so many achievements of which she could be proud. Over time though, there was a growing pall of sadness as the health of a growing number of people associated with the service declined, and all too many died.

Lesley was exhausted, and she wondered how much longer she could sustain herself – but she was also crippled by worries of what

would happen to the service if she left. So she hung in there. Her workload felt impossible, the demands relentless, the unmet needs ever present – and the growing personal toll almost an unbearable weight to carry. When Lesley left her role, she was face down.

CHAPTER 3

MINDSET: ENABLE CHANGE

What's your story? *Not* the blow-by-blow account of your experiences and the things that happened to you throughout your life. *But*, instead, the story that you tell yourself (and perhaps no one else). Your personal narrative. What you make things mean. How your experiences, your emotions, your memories and your circumstances impact on how you process the things that happen to you. How your sense of worthiness, control, helplessness, accomplishment, self and value inform the meaning you ascribe to your experiences.

As human beings, we are fundamentally makers of meaning. And most of that is an internal process in our minds.

The dialogue in our heads is perhaps the most important dialogue in our lives – and it is the one that we often allow to ramble on unchecked as it influences our energy, emotions and sense of worth. It also influences how we see ourselves, how we see others, and how we frame our circumstances. When this dialogue is negative, it causes unhelpful, and often unconscious, patterns and habits to influence us every day.

Our thoughts are absolutely real – but they might not be true. They can manifest as limiting beliefs, and can influence our emotional responses and our behaviour – and they can cause harm to ourselves and others.

One of the most important lessons I learnt in my process of recovery from burnout was how to approach my thoughts with curiosity – playfulness, even. To not give them so much power over me, and to learn that I could, quite simply, let them go and choose to change my narrative.

I recognise in retrospect that my personal narrative was limiting, that my sense of worth was disabling, and that, instead of taking responsibility for my own wellbeing, I was allowing myself to be buffeted by the choices and behaviours of others. I gave away my power and put my wellbeing in the hands of others. And the approach they took was certainly not to 'handle with care'. Turning that around wasn't up to them – it was up to me.

It is absolutely and infinitely possible to change your world – but it is up to you, and a key part of doing so is your mindset. You need to create an enabling mindset that will set you on a course in which you are in control. You need to let go of limiting beliefs, unhealthy habits, and thoughts and patterns that hold you back. As said by Carol Dweck,

> *'The passion for stretching yourself and sticking to it, even (or especially) when it is not going well, is the hallmark of the growth mindset. This is the mindset that allows people to thrive during some of the most challenging times in their lives.'*[32]

It is absolutely and infinitely possible to change your world – but it is up to you, and a key part of doing so is your mindset. You need to create an enabling mindset that will set you on a course in which you are in control. You need to let go of limiting beliefs, unhealthy habits, and thoughts and patterns that hold you back.

LET'S START THIS BUSINESS OF SHIFTING YOUR MINDSET

There are nine concepts I'd like to share with you, all of which can help you adopt and maintain a healthy and enabling mindset. They are:

1. Practise mindfulness.
2. Choose courage over fear.
3. Accept 100 per cent of personal responsibility for yourself.
4. Reframe your thoughts.
5. Let go of comparison.
6. Honour your time.
7. Let go of 'perfect' and choose 'good enough'.
8. Focus your efforts on where the greatest benefit can be derived.
9. Adopt an attitude of gratitude.

These are all practices that I discovered, learnt about, tried out, and found useful on my own path to recovery. They are also concepts that I have since integrated into my life and that I certainly turn to when challenges arise. I have also woven them into my practice when working with organisations, teams and individuals.

Each of these concepts is described in this chapter. I encourage you to complete the suggested self-reflection exercises and to take action, so that you can start to feel the difference these concepts can make in your life. Any step forward, no matter how tentative or small, will start you on your path to a better life.

PRACTISE MINDFULNESS

Mindfulness is the big kahuna.

If it was a pill, we'd all want to take it.

The evidence to support mindful meditation practice has demonstrated impacts on the brain that include more positive emotional states and less depressive or negative moods. It has also been shown to reduce the rate of relapse of depression, comparable to a maintenance dose of antidepressants. Improved immune responses and increased DNA repair have also been demonstrated, including reduced age-related damage.[33] In my personal experience, I've found mindfulness to be an antidote for burnout.

I started to meditate daily when I was really unwell. As I reflect back on that time now, I see it as a turning point. In the midst of grief and distress, chaos and confusion, this practice enabled me to find clarity, space, focus and calm. Breathing techniques helped me to sit with and work through difficult emotions. I was able to clear some of the clutter in my mind, lift the fog, and shift my relationship with my thoughts. To observe my thoughts rather than embody them, choosing to let them go if they weren't helpful instead of allowing them to spiral out of control.

I started some guided meditations in early 2015. Because it was working well, I then decided to join Mindful in May, a global mindfulness movement founded by Australian psychiatrist Elise Bialylew in 2012. This program included a meditation every day for the month of May. It provided me with the opportunity to build a daily habit and also included access to interviews with experts that progressed my learning about the science and art of mindfulness. This was the game-changing practice that enabled my recovery. What I learnt about my thoughts and emotions, how my brain works, and how I can bring calm and perspective into my life at the darkest of times has stayed with me and continues to provide benefits.

My meditation practice has transformed my sleep, helped me develop my gratitude practice, and given me a mechanism with which I can express kindness to myself and others. The loving-kindness practice was one that I discovered and that has had a particularly profound impact on my life. It includes four dimensions that are reinforced in a mantra during the meditation. You repeat this mantra to firstly show loving-kindness to yourself, secondly to a loved one, thirdly to someone you have a difficult relationship with, and finally, to a stranger:

May I feel safe and protected.

May I feel happy and peaceful.

May I feel healthy and strong.

May I live with ease.

Over time, and as I reflected on this practice and the four dimensions of the loving-kindness mantra, I came to realise that none of these four statements rang true for me as I meditated. And that they hadn't for years. This gave me a point to focus on. I decided that I would get to the point where I felt these things. All of them. At the same time! Through this practice, and applying the many practices I share in this book, I'm pleased to say that I now feel safe and protected, happy and peaceful, healthy and strong, and I feel that I live with a level of ease. Yay!

Since then, I've tried to maintain a regular mindfulness practice. I don't always meditate daily – but when I do meditate, I derive benefits every single time. And if I feel myself slipping into unwellness, this is the first thing that I turn to. Almost immediately, it starts my process of reset and aids my resilience – and I bounce back.

A mindfulness practice can support your daily life. And it doesn't have to be hard. Guided meditations are available through apps you can download on your phone. You can start with a one-minute meditation a day if you wish, and then you can build from there.

EXERCISE: REFLECT ON AND PRACTISE MINDFULNESS

To apply mindfulness to your own life, complete this two-part exercise.

1. Reflection:
Consider the loving-kindness mantra. Then, think about the answers to these questions:

- Which of these dimensions of wellness and peace do you have in your life at the moment?
- Which ones don't you have?

- What might need to change so that you have all of these dimensions of wellness and peace in your life?

2. Action:
Download a guided meditation app on your phone, search for a loving-kindness meditation, and give it a go. Explore other guided meditations and find ones that you like. Try and build a daily routine. As next May approaches, consider signing up for Mindful in May to really elevate your practice and help integrate mindfulness into your life.

CHOOSE COURAGE OVER FEAR

I would describe myself as a life-long learner. Always looking for new insights, never backing away from an opportunity to try something new, and constantly adding to my toolkit of skills and techniques. Quite early in my process of recovery, as I was re-establishing myself in my consultancy practice, I wanted to explore ways of transforming the impact that I could make through my work. I enrolled in a course designed for people running solo practices and immersed myself in learning. This was an exciting and challenging time. I was still managing my energy and wellbeing very actively on a daily basis as I continued to rebuild my life, and facing into and managing the daily challenges it presented.

At the end of the first year of the course, I met Dan Diamond, a fellow student and American physician who was on a similar path to mine with his own practice. I was interested in Dan's work and watched his TEDx talk when I returned home that day. He spoke of the characteristics of different people in times of crisis, like natural disasters. Those who stay in a safe space (he calls a box) with a stockpile of supplies to get them through. Those who, despite risk of great personal harm, peer out of their box and witness others suffering. Those who step out of their box into danger in order to offer assistance to others. This concept of being inside a box and peering out into the world outside resonated very strongly with me, particularly this quote:

> 'Is it possible that I've stockpiled enough supplies inside my box to survive but I might fail to live?'[34]

At the time, despite great intentions to step out of my comfort zone and to be more courageous with my ideas, I realised that fear was prevailing and keeping me in my box; in my comfort zone. The only way I could transform the impact I make through my work was by reaching a wider audience, and that required me to get out of my own way and step forward into my courage zone. To be vulnerable. To open myself up to criticism, rejection and failure. Dan's talk provided the impetus for me to keep moving forward as I contemplated the alternatives. The pain of rejection versus the pain of not living fully. Letting fear keep me from doing my best work *and* living my best life. After everything I had been through up to that point, that was not an option I was going to settle for.

Let's explore the comfort and courage zones a little more. And throw a little chaos into the mix.

Your comfort zone can be a lovely place to be in – but nothing grows there. It's where you're living your *status quo* life.

Your courage zone is where you grow, where you thrive, and where you learn, strive and evolve. You also dare, improve and inspire. This is where the magic happens – but it's also where you experience the greatest fear.

Beyond courage is the chaos zone. I would argue that this is a bridge too far. You are so far out of your comfort zone that you risk becoming ineffective through overwhelm and paralysis. This is where risks are high, and you are in a state of confusion and turmoil. You are more likely to be draining your energy and well-being in this zone than building reserves!

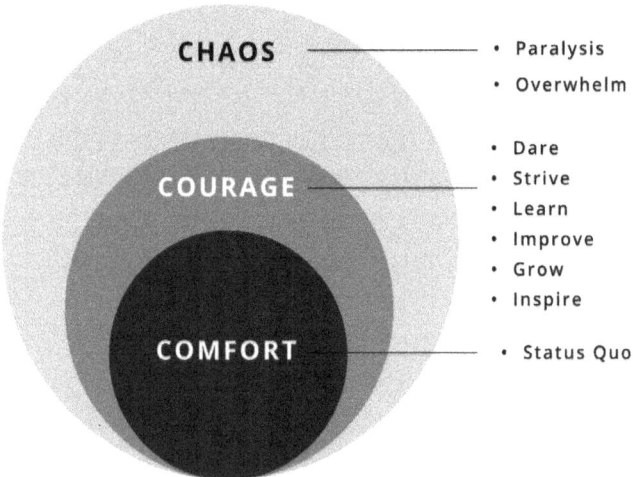

The more you are able to inhabit your courage zone, the greater progress and impact you will make in work and in life. However, operating from the courage zone requires you to get a whole lot more comfortable with fear. This is not about being fearless. It is where you feel the fear and choose to step forward anyway – out of your box.

The more you are able to inhabit your courage zone, the greater progress and impact you will make in work and in life. However, operating from the courage zone requires you to get a whole lot more comfortable with fear. This is not about being fearless. It is where you feel the fear and choose to step forward anyway – out of your box.

When you reflect back on your life, will you celebrate being careful and avoiding risk? Or will you be glad you took risks, faced into your fears, and courageously stepped forward and strived to be your best self, do your best work and live your best life?

In her book, *Big Magic*, Elizabeth Gilbert explores her relationship with fear.[35] She describes fear as being inevitable, particularly when you are daring to create a better life for yourself. Gilbert creates a metaphor in which she describes life as a road trip and fear as a constant travel companion. You can't avoid it or leave it behind. She created a mechanism to manage her fear by setting the ground rules for fear as she stepped forward in her creativity. Here's her letter to fear:

> *"Dearest Fear: Creativity and I are about to go on a road trip together. I understand you'll be joining us, because you always do. I acknowledge that you believe you have an important job to do in my life, and that you take your job seriously.*
>
> *Apparently, your job is to induce complete panic whenever I'm about to do anything interesting – and, may I say, you are superb at your job. So by all means, keep doing your job, if you feel you must.*
>
> *But I will also be doing my job on this road trip, which is to work hard and stay focused. And Creativity will be doing its job, which is to remain stimulating and inspiring. There's plenty of room in this vehicle for all of us, so make yourself at home, but understand this:*
>
> *Creativity and I are the only ones who will be making any*

decisions along the way. I recognise and respect that you are part of this family, and so I will never exclude you from our activities, but still – your suggestions will never be followed.

You're allowed to have a seat, and you're allowed to have a voice, but you are not allowed to have a vote. You're not allowed to touch the road maps; you're not allowed to suggest detours; you're not allowed to fiddle with the temperature. Dude, you're not even allowed to touch the radio.

But above all else, my dear old familiar friend, you are absolutely forbidden to drive." [35]

That is what you need to do.

You need to feel the fear and acknowledge the fear. Then, despite the fear's attempts to intervene, you need to take a step, no matter how small, towards better.

EXERCISE: CHOOSE COURAGE OVER FEAR

To apply courage to your own life, complete this two-part exercise.

1. Reflection:
Consider your answers to these questions:

- Are you stuck in your comfort zone? If so, is it truly comfortable or just less scary than the alternative?

- Does fear take a back seat, or are you letting it navigate or even drive?
- Could you change your relationship with fear? If so, how?

2. Action:
Read Elizabeth Gilbert's letter to fear, then consider how you might reframe your awareness of and response to fear. Try to be consciously aware of the role that fear is playing in your daily life. Write a simple mantra that tells fear who is actually the boss.

ACCEPT 100 PER CENT OF PERSONAL RESPONSIBILITY FOR YOURSELF

If you are struggling, could it be that you have relinquished your own power over your wellbeing to others? Accepting and enduring difficult behaviour. Dismissing the personal toll on you or those around you. Or, perhaps, you find yourself passively being buffeted by the challenges of your daily life because it all feels too hard – the challenges, constraints, workload, demands, conflict, never-ending need, and the many tasks that divert your attention daily. Maybe you have resolved that there is nothing you can do to change your situation, that this is the way of the system, your workplace, your team. That despite your early career aspirations and gallant efforts to enact meaningful change, you surrender to your powerlessness and raise the white flag. Feeling a lack of control is a risk factor for burnout.

But you are in control. You need to accept 100 per cent of personal responsibility for yourself.

Now, it's true that we need reform at every level of our society, system, workplaces and teams so that burnout is addressed adequately in the health and social sectors. That responsibility needs to be taken at all levels. I don't believe it is helpful or appropriate to place all of the onus of responsibility onto the individual. However, I *do* believe that you are the only person who can make the choice for yourself to chart a different course in your work and your life.

I learnt this the hard way. No one was coming to my rescue, so I had to rescue myself.

It's also important to set an example. We need self-determined leaders, at every level in every role, who have energy to burn, and who reject burnout as inevitable and the norm. This has to start with getting ourselves in good shape – so that we can go the distance and so that we can then influence the much-needed reforms in our sectors.

Be 100 per cent responsible for you. For the choices that you make and the consequences of those choices. For how you respond to the circumstances of your life and work, and to the behaviour of others. Accept and acknowledge this responsibility.

Do not take responsibility for the choices of others or for their behaviour. That is theirs to take responsibility for and theirs alone. By all means, provide them with feedback, raise issues and ask for what you need. They are responsible for how they respond.

EXERCISE: ACCEPT 100 PER CENT OF PERSONAL RESPONSIBILITY FOR YOURSELF

To accept 100 per cent of personal responsibility for yourself, complete this two-part exercise.

1. Reflection:
Consider your answers to these questions:

- Have you relinquished control over your own wellbeing and given it to others?
- Have you surrendered to the seeming inevitability of constraints, stress and conflict?
- Do you feel helpless and like things are beyond your control?
- Are you waiting for someone to rescue you?
- Do you need to step up and rescue yourself?
- What does taking 100 per cent of personal responsibility mean for you? What would need to change?

2. Action:
Think of something you need and ask for it today.

Pay close attention to times when you feel powerless or negatively influenced by those around you. Recognise that you have control over the choices you make in each moment, and be more mindful in how you respond and proactive in managing your wellbeing.

Be consciously aware of times when you are taking on someone else's problems. Choose to let that habit go – it doesn't serve you or them.

You are the only person who can make the choice for yourself to chart a different course in your work and your life.

I learnt this the hard way. No one was coming to my rescue, so I had to rescue myself.

It's also important to set an example. We need self-determined leaders, at every level in every role, who have energy to burn, and who reject burnout as inevitable and the norm. This has to start with getting ourselves in good shape – so that we can go the distance and so that we can then influence the much-needed reforms in our sectors.

REFRAME YOUR THOUGHTS AND SHIFT YOUR SELF-TALK

In his book, *Useful Belief* [36], Chris Helder writes about the importance of adopting a belief that is positive and useful instead of applying a negative lens, which we often use to filter our experiences and the assumptions we make about ourselves and others. It's a very simple and very freeing concept. Here's how you do it.

Choose to believe that you and you alone hold the key to your health and wellbeing. That you can create a mindset that will set you free – and that will enable you to step off that hamster wheel.

Here are five examples of how I have applied this concept in practice.

1. Catch yourself when you're thinking unhelpful thoughts. Practice letting those thoughts go. Simply notice them and then choose to let them pass.
2. If you are on a downward spiral, where you are making assumption after assumption and reaching negative conclusions, recognise that this is a narrative that is playing itself out in your head and is not the truth. Question your assumptions. Choose a 'useful belief' to stop the downward spiral – one that is more healthful and productive for you.
3. Play with language. A simple change of a word or words can completely shift your energy and emotions. I have become really conscious of words like 'should', 'can't', 'struggle' and 'busy' – and how they make me feel. The thoughts that come to mind with each word are:
    - *Should* – I have to, rules, obligations, necessity, burden

Choose to believe that you and you alone hold the key to your health and wellbeing. That you can create a mindset that will set you free – and that will enable you to step off that hamster wheel.

- *Can't* – shame, deficit, a flaw in me, a failing
- *Struggle* – stuck in a holding pattern, a lack of progress, something wrong with me, too hard, assuming it wouldn't be this hard for others
- *Busy* – everyone's busy, it's just how it is, busy shows I am committed

When I say or think these words these days, I try to catch myself, then I actively reframe my language. For example:

- Reframing 'I should' to 'I could'.
- Reframing 'I can't' to 'I need to learn how to'.
- Reframing 'I'm struggling' to 'I am finding this challenging'.
- Reframing 'I'm busy' to 'I choose to spend my time on that'.

When I do this, I find that the potency of those words is lessened. The reframing feels less burdensome, less like there's something wrong with me, and more like I am exercising choice and control. Helpful, useful and freeing.

4. Speak to yourself as if you were speaking to someone else. All too often, we are our own harshest critics. We might focus only on our failures and our perceived shortcomings – without giving ourselves the compassion we would give to anyone else who might be having a hard time. Tara Brach, a wonderful mindfulness teacher associated with Mindful in May, instructs you to put your hands on your heart and say something compassionate and kind to yourself. Something like, 'That must be so hard for you' or, 'I'm sorry for your pain'. This simple practice brings a sense of relief when the burdens of life feel too heavy to carry.

5. The final practice I want to explore here is one I used to help me shift my negative and unhelpful self-talk. This practice is simple but effective, as many of these are. First, I would draw a heart with my finger on the steamed-up mirror in my bathroom after a shower. Inside it, I would write 'I am enough.' When I would have a shower the next day and the steam would rise, the outline of the heart and the message would reappear, and I would retrace the heart and the words with my finger. It became a daily ritual – and it was easy to maintain, thanks to the poor ventilation in my bathroom!

When I started this practice, the saying I wrote on the mirror wasn't something I believed. At first, I would write the message, sometimes feeling a little anxiety as I did. When I felt this way, I would look at myself in the mirror and take a deep, calming breath. I would actively choose to believe what I had written, even if only for the duration of that breath in and out – 'I am enough.' Over time, that belief started to stick; it endured for longer. It became easier for me to choose to believe it and, with time, it became integrated as a core belief.

As my recovery continued, and my focus changed with the evolving circumstances of my life and work, I changed what I wrote in the heart to reflect another step or area of need that I had discovered. A new belief I needed to focus on and nurture until, again, I believed it myself. 'I am worthy.' 'I am beautiful.' A single reminder, once a day, that took me from being harsh and self-critical to being kind and compassionate to myself. To believing I am enough, I am worthy and, even, I am beautiful.

EXERCISE: REFRAME YOUR THOUGHTS AND SHIFT YOUR SELF-TALK

To reframe your thoughts and shift your self-talk, complete this two-part exercise.

1. Reflection:
Consider your answers to these questions:

- What do you say to yourself when you are finding things hard?
- When you do find things hard, are you kind to yourself?
- When you say these things, are they helpful or are they harsh?

2. Action:
Catch yourself when you engage in negative self-talk and when you say words and phrases to yourself that make you feel pressured, hopeless, helpless, useless, slow or simply not good enough. Be grateful that you took a moment to notice these behaviours – that's worth celebrating. Then, try actively reframing your thoughts and your words to take the sting out of them.

Reflect on the acts of self-compassion from the strategies just provided, give them a try, and create your own ritual that brings you instant relief.

LET GO OF COMPARISON

You might find yourself being envious of someone who seems to you to have it all. Secretly, you might even feel a little resentful. But what we see in others is rarely the actual truth. We are all struggling in our own ways – *everyone* is. And yet, we can be very harsh towards ourselves while looking at others with rose-coloured glasses.

I've come to recognise my feelings of resentment as a red flag for me. When I experience these feelings, I sometimes find myself thinking that someone has it easier than me – they have more wealth or more choices, or they haven't had to work as hard or had to face anywhere near the level of challenges as I have. My thoughts usually go something like, 'Well it's alright for you, you don't have to...', and end with me feeling sorry for myself. I might also feel a little shame at feeling sorry for myself because there's always people worse off than me.

I've worked out that feeling sorry for myself is very different from being kind and compassionate to myself. It's a negative state and it's sticky. I can get stuck there and, when in that place, feel justified in not taking risks or striving. Resentment keeps me in my comfort zone, not stepping into my courage zone. At a fundamental level, that is just not helpful and won't support me to step forward into better.

When I find myself feeling resentful, I now use a strategy to challenge those feelings. I call a timeout and reflect on what my feelings are *really* about. I remind myself that I have no right to compare myself with others, as guided by Rob Bell in this quotation:

> 'You have no right to compare what you know about yourself with what you don't know about someone else.'[37]

The fact is – as explored in his quotation – I don't know the truth of whomever I'm comparing myself to. Additionally, engaging in this thought process is simply not helpful. I reflect on how resentment is an emotion that keeps me small and stops me from stepping into my courageous self to make meaningful progress. I then find something I can change about what I am doing, thinking or feeling – and then I choose to find a sense of control rather than being stuck in a negative place.

Let go of comparison.

It does not serve you or anyone else.

EXERCISE: LET GO OF COMPARISON

To let go of comparison, complete this two-part exercise.

1. Reflection:
Consider your answers to these questions:

- Are there people in your life who you compare yourself to?
- If so, do you experience feelings of inadequacy or resentment when you think about them?

- If there are people in your life that you compare yourself to, do you think the assumptions you are basing those comparisons on represent the actual truth of that person's life?

2. Action:
Notice yourself when you are in 'comparison mode', or when you are filled with feelings or words of resentment. Stop. Take a breath and reflect. Recognise this as a story you are telling yourself – one that doesn't serve you and that probably isn't true. Then consider your answers to these questions:

- What issue do I need to address to move forward?
- What can I control?

Then, engage in a small action that leads you to step in the right direction.

HONOUR YOUR TIME

Consider time to be the very precious resource that it is. Use it wisely. To be crystal clear, that doesn't mean you have to work like a maniac. It means respecting the twenty-four hours you have in a day and ensuring that you are mindful about how you use those hours. This includes time for: sleep, eating, wellbeing, play and work (at home, in your place of work, and with regard to your other commitments, such as voluntary work or community service). Remember that working longer doesn't mean working better, as you will not be at your most productive if you neglect your wellbeing.

EXERCISE: HONOUR YOUR TIME

To honour your time, complete this two-part exercise.

1. Reflection:
Consider your answers to these questions:

- Do you respect, honour and value your time the way you might do for others?
- Do you let your work time bleed into and impose upon quality time with your family, leisure time, sleep, play, and doing things that bring you joy?
- Is it possible that you could set clearer boundaries around your time and still get things done?

Be honest with yourself about your level of productivity, as well as about how distracted, tired, frustrated and overwhelmed you feel – and how these factors are truly impacting on your capacity to function optimally. What if actively investing time in the things that bring you joy actually helps you be more present and productive when at work? At the very least, if you do this, you'll feel less resentful, overwhelmed and frustrated.

2. Action:
Think about how you are spending your time these days. On weekdays and weekends, day and night. For the next seven days, note down the chunks of time you spend in each twenty-four-hour period within these main categories: work, spending time with family, sleep, exercise and wellbeing, leisure, household duties

(cooking, cleaning, food shopping, household-running activities), and any other categories that are relevant to you.

At the end of the week, reflect on the amount of time spent in each category each day and over the week as a whole. Does this serve you? What could you change, if it doesn't? Consider experimenting with your schedule – such as going to bed earlier, setting clearer boundaries around work time and personal time, or committing to thirty minutes of physical activity every day. Choose one thing to experiment with, and try it for the next week. Track your time, and then reflect again at the end of that week.

Once you've done that, consider what impact the change has made on your wellbeing, your stress levels and your productivity – what you've achieved. Has it taken up precious time, or does it feel like you've freed up time and energy? Then, consider whether you will continue on with that change, and what experiment you might try for the following week. Do this until you are happy with how you spend your time every week.

LET GO OF 'PERFECT' AND CHOOSE 'GOOD ENOUGH'

We can be our own harshest critics and think that nothing we ever do is perfect. This is a result of the fact that there will always be unmet needs. No program or service is ever going to be flawless or solve all of the wicked problems we face. So it's easy to feel like we can always do better – and like we *should* always do better.

This relentless drive for perfection, however, is not the solution and *should not* be the goal. Perfectionism will, in fact, make things worse, adding to your already crippling workload pressures – and it could even be your undoing.

Remember earlier in this chapter when we discussed some of Elizabeth Gilbert's thoughts in her book, *Big Magic*? We can learn more from her here, thinking about perfectionism and how she discusses it in the same book. She describes perfectionism as a form of fear disguised as a virtue:

> *'I think perfectionism is just fear in fancy shoes and a mink coat, pretending to be elegant when actually it's just terrified. Because underneath that shiny veneer, perfectionism is nothing more than a deep existential angst that says, again and again, "I am not good enough, and I will never be good enough".'*

Instead of perfectionism, Elizabeth advocates for 'good enough'. She explains:

> *'Don't hold back your ideas until they're perfect. Because, first of all, perfect doesn't exist, and, secondly, you'll be overrun by people who are throwing out stuff that's half formed when yours is 95% formed – 95% is good enough. Done is better than good.'*

It's all too common to expend a whole lot of time and energy on that last five or ten per cent of a task. You are often fiddling with details, such as worrying about whether you have missed any final grammatical errors.

Or, you may not be at the final five per cent – instead, you might be at an early stage in a piece of work and be unsure of what to do, but perhaps feel like you should know and that you definitely need to work this out for yourself. As time passes, you remain stuck, and you feel even less confident in asking for help and, in so doing, revealing that you haven't made much progress or remain unsure as to how to even make a start. When this happens, all of the elements of this situation add to your burden and weigh you down.

It's too much. You need to lift that burden off yourself. Ask someone how they'd approach the task or bounce ideas around with a colleague. Ask for guidance from your boss or mentor. This is not weakness or inadequacy – this is effectiveness. As the work progresses, choose to aim for 'good enough'. Remind yourself as often as you need to that you are good enough, that you have put in a solid effort, and that you have done the best with the time and resources you have available.

EXERCISE: LET GO OF 'PERFECT' AND CHOOSE 'GOOD ENOUGH'

To let go of 'perfect' and choose 'good enough', complete this two-part exercise.

1. Reflection:
Consider your answers to these questions:

- Would you describe yourself as a perfectionist? If the answer is yes, do you see it as a strength or a virtue?
- If you think about sharing an idea or circulating a document that's 'good enough', do you get an uncomfortable feeling in the pit of your stomach?
- Do you think you might be stuck in a relentless pursuit of perfection that is getting in the way of your ultimate effectiveness? Is it possible that fear is playing a part in this and that perfectionism is a trap that's keeping you in your comfort zone, adding to your burden and workload, and reducing the impact of your efforts?

2. Action:
Catch yourself, next time, when you're delaying sending off a written work assignment until you've done one last re-read or when you're thinking of saying to someone, 'I just want to work on this a little longer.' Then, stop. Breathe. Ask yourself, 'Is this good enough just the way it is? What's the worst thing that could actually happen if I don't pore over it for a few more hours?' Then, put it out there, knowing you did the best you could – and enjoy the relief of ticking that task off your to-do list and moving on to something else. Be open to feedback and the need for revisions. This will feel much better than striving for perfection and then feeling demoralised when, inevitably, changes are suggested.

FOCUS YOUR EFFORTS ON WHERE THE GREATEST BENEFIT CAN BE DERIVED

Chances are, you're familiar with the eighty-twenty rule. What you may not know is that it's based on a principle, the Pareto principle, which was posited by Italian economist Vilfredo Pareto in the 1800s.[38]

In coming up with this principle, Pareto made a series of observations: that twenty per cent of pea pods produced eighty per cent of peas; that twenty per cent of houses represented eighty per cent of the housing market with respect to their value; and that twenty per cent of the world's population had eighty per cent of the wealth. The concept of the principle is that, in almost every sphere of life, there is a small collective group creating most of the output.

This phenomenon has since been observed in many other spheres. These include: twenty per cent of clouds producing eighty per cent of rain; twenty per cent of the Earth's surface producing eighty per cent of its mineral wealth and food; and eighty per cent of the Earth's energy, metal and timber that is used being consumed by twenty per cent of countries.[39]

The principle can be usefully applied to think about leverage. It is not possible to do everything and achieve everything. But what if you think about the activities you could engage in that would generate the greatest returns? The twenty per cent you could focus more time and energy on that would create an eighty per cent yield. A greater return for the investment of your time, energy and expertise than other tasks you could choose to focus on.

When you're busy and have an overwhelming workload, you might just keep powering through without stopping to think and reflect. If you did stop, just for a moment even, to think about which activities you could focus on that would result in the greatest impact or benefit, you could increase your effectiveness. Be mindful of and value your time, your energy and your expertise. Think about these as your investment and consider what the returns are on that investment.

An example is to feel like you don't have the time to train someone up to take on a responsibility. You might say to yourself, 'It's quicker to just do it myself.' So your time now is spent doing something that could be delegated. Upskilling someone else takes time upfront (an investment) but the payoff (the return) is that, once they are up to speed, you have relieved some of your burden, and you have created greater freedom, choice and capacity to focus on the work that matters most. Recognise that focusing your energy and efforts is an act of self-compassion.

EXERCISE: FOCUS YOUR EFFORTS ON WHERE THE GREATEST BENEFIT CAN BE DERIVED

To focus your efforts on where the greatest benefit can be derived, complete this two-part exercise.

1. Reflection:
Consider your answers to these questions:

- How could you use this concept to your advantage?

- Considering where your time currently goes, your to-do list and your diary, what activities represent smart investments of your time, energy and expertise – your twenty per cent that will result in the eighty per cent return? What activities could you focus your efforts and energies on that would deliver the greatest impact or those that have flow-on effects in terms of freeing up capacity?
- What could you do? What's feasible?

2. Action:
Apply the eighty-twenty rule when you're making decisions about priorities and when you're considering what work to do in the coming week or even day. Be mindful of opportunities to choose leveraged activities that you will derive the most benefit from each day and as you plan ahead. Integrate eighty-twenty thinking into your routine, and enjoy the greater impact and ease that results from it.

ADOPT AN ATTITUDE OF GRATITUDE

The final concept we will cover in this chapter is gratitude. This can be an incredibly simple practice, and there is evidence of a range of wellbeing benefits. Gratitude has been shown to safeguard against stress, and improve physical and mental health, social functioning and interpersonal relationships. It has been shown to reduce antisocial behaviour and to support resilience across the life course. Of great relevance to this book, and to work in the health and social sectors, gratitude has been shown to help

> '*individuals find greater meaning and coherence in life so that they can improve themselves and elevate others.*'[40]

Similar to when you work out and build muscle, when you adopt a routine gratitude practice, you further grow your focus on the positive.

Have you ever noticed how, when you're single, all you see is loved-up couples *everywhere*? Or perhaps you chat with a friend about buying a new red car and then you find yourself noticing red cars everywhere you look. These examples reflect the function of a neat mechanism in your brain, the reticular activating system, or RAS. There is no way we could process all of the information that enters our brain each moment through our senses. Your RAS acts like a filter and primes your brain to notice things that matter to you.[41]

Once you start focusing on what you're grateful for, this same system brings to your consciousness a greater awareness of more to be grateful for. You'll catch yourself noticing and appreciating things in the moment – things that may have previously passed you by.

Practising gratitude can be as simple as integrating a reflection practice into your routine, perhaps when you first wake in the morning and/or when you go to bed at night. Ask yourself, 'What's one thing I'm grateful for?' You might write this down, just think about it, or share it with a loved one.

When I started this practice, I was not at all well, and some days were an incredible challenge to get through. I would sit down with a little notebook at the end of the day, and I would write down three things that I was grateful for and one thing from the past twenty-four hours that had made me happy. Some days, it was, 'I'm breathing' or, 'I have a roof over my head' – the basics. Other days, it was simple moments of peace and joy, achievements and even breakthroughs. But no matter what I reflected upon and wrote, my gratitude practice was always helpful. A reminder that I was okay. A much-needed perspective. An opportunity to take a breath and feel thankful, no matter what.

I found – no matter how down I was – that if I practiced gratitude, I always felt better. It lifted my spirits, helping me shift my focus so that I noticed more of what made me happy. The beauty around me. Those small moments of happiness and love.

EXERCISE: ADOPT AN ATTITUDE OF GRATITUDE

To adopt an attitude of gratitude, complete this two-part exercise.

1. Reflection:
Consider your answers to these questions:

- Do you stop and then reflect on the things that you are grateful for? Or are you too busy, so busy that you can't stop, and all you do is go, go, go?
- Do you take a moment to celebrate your small wins or achievements by sharing the news with your colleagues, friends, partner or family?

2. Action:

Create a simple gratitude practice by putting a pen and notebook somewhere that will make it easy for you to stop, reflect, and note down three things you are grateful for. For example, you might put the notebook and pen on your bedside table, so that you practice gratitude before you go to bed at night – or next to your kettle, so that you can do your practice while you are waiting for the kettle to boil when making your morning cuppa. When doing your gratitude practice, think about the past twenty-four hours and note down three things you are grateful for. Once you've written them, sit for a moment or two, take a deep breath, and enjoy the feeling of gratitude.

CREATING 'POSSIBLE'

All of the concepts and practices provided in this chapter will help you make 'possible' the seemingly impossible situations you find yourself in. These concepts and practices will take you from feeling helpless, hopeless or like you have little control to feeling more present and focused. They will also help you make more conscious choices and provide you with much-needed relief – even if that much-needed relief lasts only a few moments. These moments are addictive, and the more you practice the concepts covered in this chapter, the better you will feel. It will also be easier for you to shift to a positive mindset that enables positive change in your work and in your life.

It's time for you to start empowering yourself with concepts and practices like these, and building your wellbeing on your terms.

It's time for you to start empowering yourself with concepts and practices like these, and building your wellbeing on your terms.

EXERCISE: CREATING 'POSSIBLE'

To create 'possible' by using this chapter's concepts and practices, consider your answers to these questions:

- Which of these concepts and practices were you aware of or have already tried?
- Which of these concepts and practices are you considering testing to see whether they might be something to add to your own personal wellbeing toolkit?
- What do you have to lose?
- What might you gain?

BURNOUT FACTS #4

WORKPLACES THAT CONTRIBUTE TO OUR DECLINE

At the workplace level, the system pressures highlighted earlier filter through and manifest in a range of ways. There is no question that some workplace environments and cultures are healthier than others. A series of factors at the workplace level influence how we cope with our work, and the toll it takes on us personally and collectively. These can be grouped into six dimensions: workload, control, reward, community, fairness and values.[42]

WORKLOAD

Workload pressures are a fundamental issue associated with burnout, placing pressure on the individual that can often be beyond their capacity to manage effectively. Workload issues are influenced by: funding and associated models of care, staffing levels (number, mix of disciplines, level of expertise and experience), how workloads are managed, and organisational culture and norms. Pressure may be placed on individual personnel to take on additional loads to manage demand. Long hours and significant unpaid overtime may be the rule rather than the exception. When a workplace has workforce shortages, or a high level of staff turnover or absenteeism, this places additional pressure on the personnel that are there to 'pick up the slack', further adding to the burden of their workload.

A commonly cited issue is the increasing and often conflicting workload demands created by onerous administrative tasks, increasing computerisation, meeting quality and safety management requirements, and contributing to the wider field, sector and profession. While all of these things are important for good governance and practice – and for a culture of improvement and excellence – when we are under pressure, they can contribute to workloads that are beyond our capacity to manage.

When people are drawn to the health sector with a desire to help others, often what is valued is the contact with individual patients or clients. When there is an increasing shift towards tasks that are not linked to meaning and purpose for an individual, this can be experienced as conflict and a source of great frustration, contributing to both exhaustion and ill feeling within the workplace.

CONTROL

The level of autonomy or control that people feel at work is an important factor that can predispose, or protect against, burnout.

When people feel valued and supported, and are enabled to work autonomously, the sense of satisfaction in their work is increased. When they feel less enabled to take responsibility or exercise judgement, frustrations grow and they can become disenfranchised from their workplace. This can flow through to challenging behaviours, to disconnection and also to a loss of self-confidence.

REWARD
Being seen, heard, acknowledged and valued is another fundamental factor. This can be in regard to the level of remuneration or benefits, working conditions and job security. It can also be related to workplace practices around pressure and demands – and recognition of the efforts that are made.

Sustained extraordinary efforts may go overlooked and unacknowledged if working at full capacity is the norm, demand remains relentless, and the pressure for more with less or the same is a constant. And, of course, there's always more to do. More demand to meet. People who don't have access to services. People who are disadvantaged. Intractable, troublesome problems that we are unable to fix. Without recognition and rewards for our efforts, we can feel like we are not valued – and this may result in us feeling resentful towards our employer and colleagues. On the flip side, we may feel like we are not doing enough, and may spiral into a sense of helplessness and hopelessness.

COMMUNITY
The sense of community within a workplace is an important part of protecting against burnout. When relationships are strong, positive, collegiate and supportive, there can be joy and humour in the daily work we do that alleviates some of the inherent strains

and stressors we face. When people are experiencing burnout, the sense of community and collegiality is eroded. As stress takes its toll, tempers fray, people withdraw, cynicism and resentment increase, and conflict can arise. For those affected and those around them, the sense of joy and fun they may have previously felt may no longer be present.

Burnout erodes our confidence and our energy. It diminishes an individual's ability to focus or to make decisions, and it can manifest through errors, absenteeism, disconnection, poor communication and apathy. Frustrations can emerge as team members feel like they are carrying the load for others who are not 'pulling their weight'. As errors occur, complaints are made and conflict emerges, we can be pulled into a distracting and draining spiral as a team and as an organisation. The workplace culture can become diminished or even toxic – and this can further potentiate the burnout experiences of those who are suffering, and may also contribute to decline in others. Working in this environment – and managing the personnel and challenges that arise – adds even more burden to our limited time and energy. As a result, we can feel like we are even further away now from meaningful work.

FAIRNESS

Feeling like you are being treated fairly is important to workplace wellbeing. This often relates to how the demands, workload and other pressures that are placed on you balance against the conditions of your employment (paid and unpaid hours, salary level, flexibility, or other provisions to support you in work and in life). Feeling that there is a reasonable balance between the demands of your work and the rewards you derive from it is important.

The concept of fairness also relates to the extent to which an organisation takes responsibility for the wellbeing of its workforce. Does responsibility for stress management fall to the individual, or is the organisation mindful, focused and proactive in alleviating stress and burden, and promoting and supporting wellbeing? Finally, fairness can be shown in the interplay between the treatment of members of the wider community, such as patients, carers and clients, and the treatment of the workforce. When issues arise or there are complaints, employees may be treated with empathy and compassion, and afforded support – or they may not.

VALUES

Most organisations have a set of values that they proudly display within their workplace and report to their community. And there are other values and norms that may prevail in the workplace culture, and behaviours that are supported, promoted and celebrated. The alignment of those values with the personal values of the individuals who work in the organisation is important. Otherwise, when there is a conflict in values, this creates a pressure point where burnout can manifest. This can be particularly so in workplaces where the espoused values may be seen as tokenistic and not implemented in practice, or when there is an evident mismatch between values and behaviours. This can undermine trust and erode wellbeing in the workplace.

A CAUTIONARY TALE

THE MINDSET TRAPS WE SET FOR OURSELVES

Here's what happens when you don't actively create 'possible'.

Louise works in a busy organisation that is funded to make game-changing progress in a major public health area. The members of her team are working towards ambitious goals and often find themselves under a lot of scrutiny. With competition for funding being like an extreme sport, cynicism and resentment often run high among the stakeholders, who all operate under financial constraints similar to those in the rest of the health and social sectors.

The organisation's staff are under a lot of pressure to deliver, and the need to outlast and outperform all expectations has become embedded into the organisational DNA. A culture of overwork has been created. Long hours, relentless pressure and unrealistic expectations have become the norm. Sometimes, impossible goals are set. These are beyond aspirational – they are just not possible.

Louise feels enormous pressure to work well beyond her allocated hours. It has now become the norm for Louise to work far longer than a standard workday – not just every now and again, but every day. She arrives in the office very early. Despite working more than her allocated hours, she also routinely works after her children are in bed – and, despite her best intentions, often finds herself dialling in to teleconferences, clearing emails, or doing work on priority projects on days off and weekends. And this is a standard

week. When deadlines are approaching or additional demands are placed on the team (which is often), Louise feels pressure to do even more – and puts that pressure on herself.

Lately, Louise has been feeling overwhelmed at work. Louise is stuck in a cycle of comparison and feels that she is simply not good enough. That she is an imposter in the role she is in among a team of people she considers much better-qualified for the task they face together.

She constantly worries what people think and always assumes the worst. Even when asked to complete what she knows is an impossible task, Louise is reluctant to raise this as an issue, as this further highlights to her that she might not be able to do it. 'Not good enough, not enough.'

I wonder how unique Louise is in her experiences and her thoughts, and how they manifest.

What resonates in this story for you? What would you do to remedy these problems?

CHAPTER 4

ENERGY: BUILD YOUR RESERVES

> *'I'm late, I'm late! For a very important date! No time to say "hello", goodbye, I'm late, I'm late, I'm late!'*
> – THE WHITE RABBIT, ALICE IN WONDERLAND [43]

How often have you responded to the question 'How are you?' with, 'Oh, you know, busy, busy, busy'? It can be easy to get caught up in our culture of 'busy'.

Not enough hours in the day.
Always more to do.
The more you do, the more your to-do list grows.
It feels relentless.
Overwhelming.
And oh, so exhausting.

THE PROBLEM OF BUSY, BUSY, BUSY

The problem with being busy, busy, busy?

When you're stuck on that hamster wheel, you can easily lose the connection you have to the meaning that inspired you to take that job or choose that career path in the first place. You're also at risk of losing the satisfaction you hoped to derive from meaningful work. And yet, despite this, it's all too easy to give too much importance to the hours you put into your work. Hours spent physically in the workplace, and time spent outside of work hours progressing your work or catching up on it. Why do people do this? It might be that, in our society, investing many hours in work is linked to having a strong work ethic. It's a sign that we truly care.

But when busy is the norm, it's only a matter of time before you start feeling resentful of the hours you're working or the value you're deriving in return. This is because of the personal energy you're investing in your work. This is even more likely to happen if what's expected of you is too much, and if your standard workload is relentless and impossible to complete without you spending long hours on the job.

But it's not just the high expectations and endless hours that will make you feel resentful – it's also the encroachment of work on other parts of your life such as time with family, downtime for rest and recreation, or time to pursue personal interests. The impact of your working so much on your partner and family – who increasingly feel like they come a poor second – will also make you feel resentful towards the hours you're working.

Being too busy can affect your mood, energy and sense of wellbeing – and it can create a vicious cycle in which, despite the hours you're putting in, you're less productive because you're less focused and less present. This just adds more workload pressure as less things are being ticked off your to-do list and, I expect, there's no shortage of new things added to the list.

You simply cannot be so busy that you don't take care of yourself! Taking care of yourself is, in fact, the most important action you can take to stop the decline to burnout. It's fundamental to providing the fuel you need to sustain your best work *and* live your best life – uncompromised.

You know that self-care is important for you and for others.

I did too!

When you work in the health and social sectors, you can be notoriously bad at taking the advice you readily give to others.

But now, it's time to take a dose of your own medicine.

It's time to build your energy and wellbeing reserves to optimise the impact you make, and minimise the personal toll on your wellbeing and your life.

ARE WE MAKING IT HARDER THAN IT NEEDS TO BE?

Hard work and sacrifice have both been parts of the storyline that has played itself out in the personal narrative of my life. Going above and beyond was always the norm for me. Serving others was a way of showing my dedication and commitment through my work and in my life.

You simply cannot be so busy that you don't take care of yourself! Taking care of yourself is, in fact, the most important action you can take to stop the decline to burnout. It's fundamental to providing the fuel you need to sustain your best work *and* live your best life – uncompromised.

However, my system was completely out of kilter. My energy and wellbeing reserves were in a state of constant drain. I didn't focus on growing, or even place value on *building*, my reserves unless I became really unwell or was forced to stop. I was, clearly, on a path to face down. And I expect I wasn't such a great role model to my teams in terms of supporting them to make positive choices about self-care. I expect I sent a resounding message to the contrary through my actions.

Being relentlessly busy is bad for your own health, and for the health and culture of your teams and workplaces.

It's not sustainable – and it's just not smart.

How so?

Let's look at how that vicious cycle might play itself out in a workplace, in the following section.

THE VICIOUS CYCLE OF BEING BUSY

The vicious cycle looks like this, with the first step being exhaustion and the last one being...repeating and starting the cycle all over again.

The flow-on effect of the first step, and then the second, is that many individuals eventually do not tend to their self-care, becoming increasingly exhausted and, ultimately, disconnected. This is a significant effect. It adds further resource constraints to an already-constrained environment, which then contributes to the decline of others.

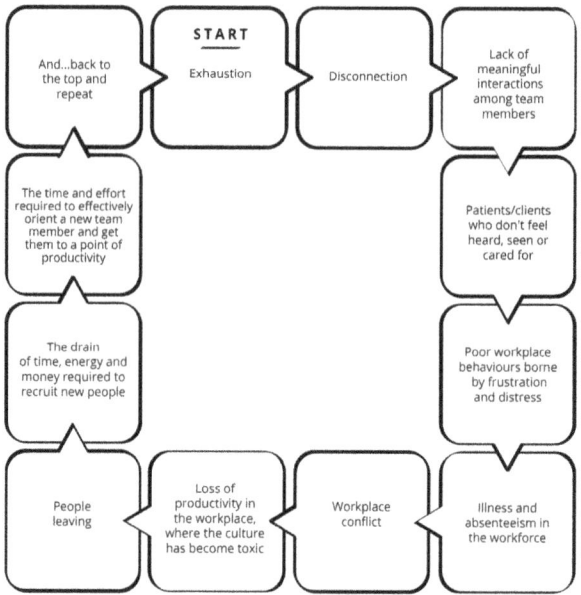

I wonder if looking at this vicious cycle diagram makes you think a bit differently about working around the clock – and about how doing so may make it impossible for you to work any harder than you already are, or may cause you to become a part of the toxicity that is plaguing our workplaces.

A SHIFT IN FOCUS FROM TIME TO ENERGY

More time spent engaged in work does not necessarily mean more output. It certainly does not mean greater quality of the outputs generated. It could serve you for a time when you have a major deadline, but it is not a 'business as usual' strategy that is likely to be effective or that you will be able to sustain. What is effective and sustainable?

Shifting your focus from time to energy.

All time is not equal. The quality of focus, clarity, attention and productivity differs according to a range of factors, including your energy levels, your emotions and other distractions. It is important to consider time and energy in tandem. When do you achieve the most in your workday? When does your energy lag and focus wane? What are the tasks you can do anytime and what are the ones that require you to be at your best? If you honour, respect and reclaim your energy – and support those around you to do the same – you might just see a transformation in yourself, in others, in your team and workplace, *and* in what you are able to achieve and sustain.

Our default position can be that there are *simply not enough hours in the day*. That the solution is to just add more time into the system by working longer hours, sleeping less, doing more, being more. Spending more time engaged in work does not equate to greater productivity or outputs. If you mindfully plan how you will invest your time and energy, how you will replenish your reserves and how you will optimise your wellbeing along the way, you will be more effective in the time you have available.

Once I focused on growing my energy and resilience, improving my coping strategies and taking greater care of myself, it felt like time expanded. I was able to achieve more in a shorter period of time. I could sustain focus instead of getting distracted by emotions that used to scramble my brain and lessen my confidence. Overwhelm and worry lessened their hold on me, and I was able to find a sense of flow.

To shift your focus from time to energy, you need to build your energy and wellbeing reserves.

In the rest of this chapter, we'll review the steps you'll want to take to build your energy and wellbeing reserves. These steps include stopping or stemming the drain and increasing the in-flows.

STOP OR STEM THE DRAIN: START HERE

There's no question that building your reserves of energy and wellbeing is essential in order to avoid decline. So, let's return to the bucket analogy. You need to focus on the ways you can make the shift from 1) Draining to 2) Balance of in-flows and out-flows to 3) A state in which you have the necessary energy and wellbeing reserves to draw on when you need them.

It's smart as a first step to explore the ways you can stop (eliminate) or stem (reduce) the drain. Of course, you can focus on increasing the in-flows – but if you're adding to a bucket with lots of holes in it, it's going to be difficult to feel like you are making meaningful progress towards wellness.

Depending on the nature of the drainers and the impact on your energy and wellbeing, you can identify areas of focus where you could stop or stem the drain by, for example:

- Prioritising action on drainers you can control
- Reducing unhealthful habits that provide merely short-term relief

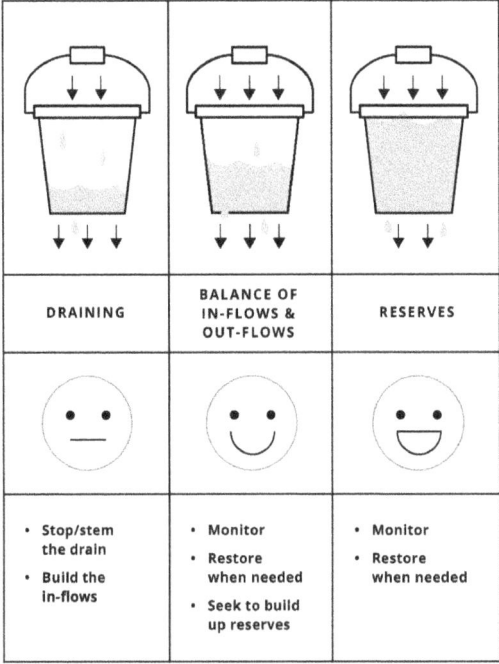

There will be drainers you can control and drainers that are beyond your control. Other people's behaviour or choices, for example, are not something you can control – beyond giving feedback and asking for change. What you can control, within this example, is the time you spend with that person, the way you think and feel about their behaviour, how you let it affect you, what you make it mean, and how you respond. You can also set boundaries about what is acceptable to you and what is not. Know and communicate what you are asking from them, maintain the boundaries as needed, and own your choices.

Here's another example. There might be a difficult situation that you have been avoiding because it feels like it would be difficult to face it. It may require you to have a difficult conversation with a colleague, for example. This could be a source of stress and discomfort – a drainer for you. But the issue remaining unresolved could also be a drain. It might be that choosing to take action is the only way to stem that flow. It might take some energy and time in the interim – but it would be an investment in your longer-term wellbeing once resolved.

Let's turn now to reducing unhealthful habits that provide merely short-term relief.

When you're struggling, there might be behaviours you adopt to help you cope with, or even numb the pain of, difficult emotions you might be experiencing. Some examples include drinking alcohol, withdrawing socially, comfort eating, and buying things you don't need with money you don't have to spare. The list can go on and on. While these habits might provide some short-term relief, they further add to the drain – so finding other, more healthful ways of coping will ultimately contribute to stemming the drain.

EXERCISE: STOP OR STEM THE DRAIN

To stop or stem the drain, complete this two-part exercise.

1. Reflection:
Think about the things that drain your energy and wellbeing as the holes in your bucket. For each drainer, consider your answers to these questions:

- Which holes could you plug to eliminate the drain altogether – and how would you do so?
- Which holes could you make smaller by reducing the energy you expend on the behaviour or the meaning you place on the source of the drain?
- What is within your control, and what is outside of your control?
- Are you setting boundaries that are healthy for you? If so, are you communicating and maintaining those boundaries?
- Are you saying yes when you should be saying no?
- Could letting go of things outside of your control free up time, energy and focus to deal with things you do have control over?
- Are there numbing behaviours you are adopting as coping mechanisms that are adding to the drain? Which of these could you eliminate or reduce?

2. Action:

Based on your reflections, write down a list of simple actions that you can take to eliminate or reduce the drains on your energy and wellbeing. Try implementing one or more of these actions in practice, and see what happens and how that makes you feel. Go about your day with a greater conscious awareness of your energy levels and how you are feeling, and take action when needed to bring relief. Revisit your reflection and action list periodically to reflect on progress made – and to identify new actions to take to keep you on track.

Tune in to your feelings when you're asked to take on

another task or responsibility – is your reaction to feel energised, or do you feel a pit in your stomach and the rise of anxiety in your chest? If you react negatively, consider saying no. Contemplate the worst outcome that could occur if you were to say no. For example, 'I'll be sacked on the spot.' Consider how likely it is that this consequence would occur. And then, if you want to say no, actually say, 'No' – and see how that feels and what happens.

INCREASE THE IN-FLOWS: THE NEXT STEP

There are a host of ways you can build up your energy and wellbeing reserves. Think of it as opening the tap that fills your bucket. Here we explore three key areas of focus:

1. BUILD YOUR ENERGY:
    - Meditate (be mindful)
    - Breathe deeply (find calm in the moment)
    - Exercise (get active)
    - Eat well (nourish your body)
    - Rest (sleep well and restore)

2. TAKE CONTROL OF YOUR TIME:
    - Get the balance of urgency and importance right
    - Work in short, sharp bursts to optimise your focus and productivity
    - Choose your number one
    - Listen to audiobooks

3. GET PLAYFUL WITH TINY HABITS:
- Prioritise a simple gratitude practice
- Smile
- Carry out simple acts of self-compassion
- Practise power and victory poses
- Work on your mental agility
- Engage in random acts of kindness

Now, we'll explore each of these ideas further. These all reflect practices that I have found invaluable in supporting my recovery and in how I actively work to maintain my wellbeing in my daily life now.

BEFORE WE GO ON: A NOTE ON OVERWHELM…

Think about the following ideas as a set of tools that you can try out and choose to put into your toolkit. Some might work, others may not. Avoid adding them all to your to-do list, which would create even more overwhelm than you already feel. Right now, the most important thing to do is to review the options presented and reflect on those that resonate with you. Don't take it all too seriously – but do make a note of things that appeal to you and that you think you might like to try. Later, we will focus on creating your personal impact plan, and, in that process, you will select and commit to a few actions.

I. BUILD YOUR ENERGY

Here's an overview of the five ways to build your energy.

MEDITATE (BE MINDFUL)
Meditation is an incredibly powerful bucket filler, as it helps you enable a healthy mindset – and, as we have previously explored, it also increases your energy and focus.

A daily practice is better than an ad-hoc one.

More is better than less.

Any is better than nothing.

Every time you do this, you will derive benefits.

EXERCISE: BUILD YOUR ENERGY BY MEDITATING

To build your energy by meditating, complete this two-part exercise.

1. Reflection:
Think about the following questions:

No time to meditate? What if, when you meditate, you clear your head and liberate your energy and focus? What if things don't take as long to do or feel less burdensome? Now is it sounding like it's worth a try?

2. Action:
Download a guided meditation app like Insight Timer or Smiling Mind, and try out meditations of different lengths and with different themes. If you find yourself struggling during the day, put your headphones on and try a one-minute meditation to reset, reduce the noise in your head, and get rid of the unhelpful emotions that are getting in the way of your meaningful progress. If you feel you are benefiting from this practice, try and create a regular practice – and consider participating in the Mindful in May campaign next May to take it to the next level and reap the rewards that it will bring.

BREATHE DEEPLY (FIND CALM IN THE MOMENT)
While deep breathing is often included as a core part of meditation practice, it can also be relaxing and calming as a practice on its own. Conscious, deep and rhythmic breathing has impacts on your brain and central nervous system. It has been shown to result in improved emotional control and psychological wellbeing. This includes an increasing sense of comfort, relaxation, pleasantness, vigour and alertness, and decreasing symptoms of arousal, anxiety, depression, anger and confusion.[44]

Apps such as Breathe Well can guide you through breathing exercises that are as short as a minute or as long as you like. Once you become more attuned to your breathing, you can implement simple strategies at any time, day or night, to bring you calm and help settle difficult emotions.

I recall standing at a city traffic light once, waiting to cross the road, and noticing a feeling of anxiety rising up in my chest and into my throat following a stressful situation at work. My mind did its thing and unhelpful negative thoughts started to spiral. Now, things are different for me. That doesn't happen anymore. These days, as soon as I notice this sort of discomfort, I take a very deep breath in, hold it for a few seconds, and then breathe out through my mouth. The anxiety lessens, I feel calmer, and I am able to refocus and keep moving. Most importantly, I stop catastrophising – nothing is ever as difficult as I imagine it is or could be.

Interestingly – and helpfully – once I started actively breathing my way through stressful situations, my reticular activating system kicked in and I started noticing other people doing it too. I would see someone taking a deep breath and breathing out through their mouth as they went about normal activities like supermarket shopping or before walking into a meeting. Adopting a useful belief, I chose to believe that they were using the same technique because, in that moment, that person was feeling anxiety. This helped me feel like I was not alone – and that I was just as 'normal' as those around me.

I encourage you to look at breathing exercises as a simple way to add to your bucket – and to also reduce the drain by managing the physical and emotional impacts of the situations you encounter along your way.

EXERCISE: BUILD YOUR ENERGY BY BREATHING DEEPLY

To build your energy by breathing deeply, complete this two-part exercise.

1. Reflection:
Consider your answers to the following questions:

When you've had a challenging encounter or felt you were under a lot of pressure, did you find your mind spiralling with unhealthy thoughts?

Do stress responses or anxiety overtake your capacity to function fully and stay present at times?

Does your mind sometimes take you straight to the worst-case scenario, running express, rushing through other stops on the way there?

2. Action:
The next time you notice yourself feeling tense, stressed, anxious or overwhelmed, observe the feeling and acknowledge it. Take a long, deep breath in, hold it for a few seconds, and then slowly breathe out, focusing on the breath until you feel empty. Repeat this two or three times until you feel calmer, more grounded, and able to refocus and regroup. Download an app such as Breathe Well to guide you in adopting some simple breathing techniques that you can add to your morning or evening routine – or fit into small gaps in your day to help you maintain your sense of wellbeing.

EXERCISE (GET ACTIVE)

The benefits of exercise are incredible – and the more you do it, the more benefits you gain. Exercise helps you maintain a healthy body weight, reduces blood pressure, decreases the risk of developing many diseases, increases muscle and bone strength and function, improves brain health and improves your mental health. It has been shown to reduce mortality from all causes. Any exercise is better than none, with regular moderate to vigorous exercise having a greater impact. The more you do the better, and that stands regardless of age and stage of life, across all ethnicities, and people with chronic conditions or disabilities.[45]

In terms of your daily life, it can add energy to your day and help you avoid energy slumps that get in the way of your being present and productive. It also contributes to the quality of your sleep. It has been shown to keep thinking, learning and judgement skills sharp, and improves mood. Makes it harder to argue you have no time to exercise, right?

You can chunk your exercise down into bite-sized pieces if you need to, and it can be as simple or as complex as you choose. You can do it for a few minutes or as long as you would like. And there are plenty of options. A walk, stretches, a bike ride, a workout at the gym, yoga, a gentle exercise routine such as qigong...the list goes on. There are plenty of guided workouts online that are free and that can be as quick as a few minutes.

Start small. Enjoy the energy that will flow through you as well as the benefits to your body and your mind. Enjoy the strengthening of your abilities to focus and to achieve. And be sure to have the right objectives when it comes to exercise. When I link exercise to goals like weight loss, I find that I can lose momentum. But when I frame exercise as an investment in my wellbeing, in sustaining my energy, and in making me a better mum and a better person – who is more present, and more in service to my family and my work – then I can sustain it.

EXERCISE: BUILD YOUR ENERGY WITH EXERCISE

To build your energy with exercise, complete this two-part exercise.

1. Reflection:
Think about the following questions.

Do you feel like you don't have time to exercise? Do you equate exercise with a gym membership and therefore worry about whether it's good value for money? When you do have time, do you find that the motivation to exercise is not forthcoming because you just want to chill out on the couch and relax?

What if doing a little exercise each day – or a few times a week – actually helped you cope with the challenges of your work and your life, gave you energy, and enabled you to enjoy the things you love more? It could be cheap or free – and exercising even just a little is better than not doing it at all. If you reframe exercise as an investment in your wellbeing, your energy, your focus and your life – and you then think about the forms of exercise you would enjoy doing – does making it happen now feel a little easier?

2. Action:
Commit to doing more exercise. Choose activities that you will enjoy – perhaps ones that you can do with someone else so that you also get the benefits that come from spending quality time with someone you love. Some examples like this include a walk with a friend to a café on the weekend, walking the dog every day, and a thirty-minute guided yoga routine that you do once a week. Mix up your exercise routine with different activities, then celebrate and track your successes.

EAT WELL (NOURISH YOUR BODY)

Unhealthy eating habits can emerge when you are struggling with maintaining your wellbeing and energy. This might be because you are eating on the run to help manage your time – or you might be skipping meals because you're 'too busy'. Unhealthy cycles can result in you buying fast food or shopping at the supermarket when you're hungry (always a bad idea for me!). You might also be turning to comfort food in an effort to make yourself feel better. And while that might seem like a good idea at the time, it isn't. In my experience, I rarely end up feeling better afterwards (in my body or in my mind).

I understand why you might be hesitating to eat well. After all, this can feel like another time/energy trade. But the extra time that goes into planning meals, shopping for what you need, and preparing healthy food is paid back to you in the added energy and wellbeing that result. You don't get the payoff without the effort.

EXERCISE: BUILD YOUR ENERGY BY EATING WELL

To build your energy by eating well, complete this two-part exercise.

1. Reflection:
Consider your answers to the following questions:

- Could your current eating habits be contributing to drains on your energy and wellbeing?
- Could a change in your diet, even in a very small way, be a bucket filler worth considering?
- Could you reframe your relationship with food by seeing it as a fuel source, and with food preparation by seeing it as an act of service and love for your family and yourself?

2. Action:
Each week, eliminate or reduce something unhealthy from your diet and replace it with something healthful. If you love cooking, explore new recipes – and consider the preparation of healthy, nourishing food as a gift to yourself and to your loved ones. If you don't love cooking, consider simple meal ideas with a few fresh ingredients that you can prepare in a short amount of time (there's plenty online) – or consider options where meal planning is done for you.

REST (SLEEP WELL AND RESTORE)

For as long as I can remember, I have had an adversarial relationship with sleep. I would describe myself as someone who has always been an insomniac. I can remember how, when I was a child, it would take me several hours to settle down to sleep. Switching my brain off was not something that came naturally, and I was not really aware for most of my life of the game-changing impact of a good night's sleep – until I had started my path to recovery from burnout.

Before that time, I had tried to improve my sleep. I'd read books about it and tried different techniques but without success. I had given up, coming to the conclusion that this was a chronic issue and that I would just need to live with it.

As I was on my path to recovery, and newly committed to my health, I discovered Arianna Huffington's book, *Thrive*.[46] In *Thrive*, Arianna talks of her own 'wake-up call', which happened when she literally collapsed from exhaustion in her office one night, hitting her head on a table on her way down and waking to find herself in a pool of her own blood on the floor. In *Thrive*, and in her subsequent writing and talks, Arianna passionately advocates for sleep as a fundamental key to wellbeing and success, and, in fact, essential for the proper functioning of our brain through the important processing work the brain does during the portion of our sleep that is spent in deep and in dreamy (rapid eye movement or REM) sleep states.

Through other practices that I had adopted already as I tried to improve my wellbeing – mostly exercise and meditation – I started to sleep better. The result? The better I slept, the better I felt.

So these days, I pay much more mindful attention to my sleep, and I use a fitness-tracking device that gives me an analysis of my sleep patterns, which I find helpful. If I am struggling to settle my thoughts at bedtime, I put on a guided sleep meditation. I have a few saved now that work for me. It's very rare that I am awake to hear the end of it. If sleep is an issue for you, I would highly recommend guided sleep meditations as a tool for improvement.

Again, the time/energy exchange comes into play. Before prioritising my sleep, I had routinely traded sleep for extra time, going to bed late or getting up super-early to create more time in my day. There's never enough hours in the day, right? Wrong! If I didn't have enough good-quality sleep, comprised of time asleep, enough deep sleep and REM sleep, then I ended up being less focused, productive and effective. I ended up losing way more hours this way, and my continual state of exhaustion was damaging to my wellbeing, lowered my resilience, and decreased my capacity to cope with daily challenges I faced.

EXERCISE: BUILD YOUR ENERGY BY RESTING

To build your energy by resting, complete this two-part exercise.

1. Reflection:
Consider your answers to these questions:

- What are you trading sleep for?

- How many hours of sleep are you getting on average? Are you sleeping well during those hours?
- Do you wake up feeling rested and ready to take on the new day?
- Could improving your sleep habits improve your life?

2. Action:
Try creating new sleep habits. Think about the times you go to bed and wake up, and how changing those times might create more hours of restful sleep. Think about your bedtime routine. Do you go to bed stressed, ruminating over things and struggling to settle into sleep? Identify some ways you can change that: read or listen to music before bedtime, drink a soothing decaffeinated tea, do some stretches or other exercises that help your body relax, or consider a guided sleep meditation. If you have a fitness-tracking device, pay attention to the sleep statistics it creates. Which are the days that you wake up feeling energised and refreshed? How many hours of sleep do you need? What influences the quality of your sleep? Try out some different techniques and go with what works for you.

2. TAKE CONTROL OF YOUR TIME

There's a series of little hacks that I've adopted that have helped me change my relationship with time. Changing my relationship with time has helped me be more productive within the hours I have available and with the energy that I have at my disposal (which at times was not much!). It has also helped me find a sense of ease and flow in situations where I previously struggled because I was hardwired for struggle.

The little hacks that helped me change my relationship with time really worked for me. Here are some you might like to play with.

GET THE BALANCE OF URGENCY AND IMPORTANCE RIGHT

Stephen Covey developed a model that shows what tasks can look like in relation to two dimensions: urgency and importance.[47] He separated tasks into four quadrants, as shown here.

URGENCY

IMPORTANCE	I URGENT AND IMPORTANT	II NOT URGENT BUT IMPORTANT
	III URGENT BUT NOT IMPORTANT	IV NOT URGENT AND NOT IMPORTANT

COVEY'S TIME MANAGEMENT MATRIX[47]

Sorting the tasks in your long to-do list according to urgency and importance can be a great technique to help reduce overwhelm. It can also be a useful mechanism for building greater awareness of your time. Having this awareness will improve the quality of your time, helping you highlight opportunities where you can shift your focus, building your energy as a result.

Quadrant I tasks are urgent and important, and they need to be prioritised. Recognise that these tasks will be harder to focus on and complete in a timely way if you are distracted, tired or anxious. Not making meaningful progress on these tasks is also likely to increase stress levels. Think about prioritising these tasks for early in the day, when you are feeling fresher. Consider blocking out time in your diary to work on these tasks – and turning off your phone and not checking your email (if you are able to) to enable greater focus during this time.

Quadrant II tasks are important but *not* urgent. These tasks are the strategic work or important projects that you often don't get to as other priorities get in the way. This lack of time spent on Quadrant II tasks can be a significant source of frustration, and may hamper you in making progress that feels and is meaningful. Making progress on a Quadrant II task is likely to make you feel a sense of accomplishment. Think about elevating one of your Quadrant II items higher on your to-do list and committing a small amount of time each day to making some progress with it.

Quadrant III tasks are *not* important, but they have a deadline or a sense of urgency to them. This often happens because someone else considers them urgent and may be applying pressure on you to complete them. But these time-pressured distractions are taking you away from more meaningful work. Are they really urgent? Is there an opportunity to discuss the sense of urgency so that you can renegotiate timeframes, making it so that completing the tasks is not at the expense of making progress on more important priorities?

Quadrant IV tasks are those that add very little, if any, value to your work. They are distractions without inherent meaning or value, and should be completed when you are taking a break from time-pressured activities or work that requires deep thinking. Things like checking emails or browsing the internet. Try catching yourself when you find yourself spending time on Quadrant IV tasks – and think about whether this is an opportunity to instead fill your bucket by taking a walk, getting some fresh air, stretching or meditating. To do something that can restore your wellbeing and focus, rather than drain your time and energy further.

EXERCISE: TAKE CONTROL OF YOUR TIME BY GETTING THE BALANCE OF URGENCY AND IMPORTANCE RIGHT

To take control of your time by getting the balance of urgency and importance right, complete this two-part exercise.

1. Reflection:
Think about the urgency and importance of each task that consumes your time and energy at work. Start with reflecting on the past week. To do this, consider your answers to these questions:

- When were the times that you got frustrated because you were very busy but didn't feel like you were making progress that was meaningful – or like

you weren't able to work on the things that matter the most to you?
- What tasks did you engage in that felt like someone else's priority – but not yours?
- Were there times that you got caught up in tangential activities that weren't value adding?

2. Action:
At the start of each day, or at the end of the prior day – whenever you prefer to stop and reflect on what you need to do for that day or the following – create a long list of what you hope to achieve. Then, add two columns beside the list – labelled 'urgent' and 'important' – and tick each task according to whether it is urgent and/or important. In a fourth column, classify each task according to whether it sits in Quadrant I, II, III or IV in the Covey model. Prioritise your Quadrant I and II tasks, and on making progress on those as best you can, before turning to Quadrant III and IV tasks. Consider having a conversation about the urgency of Quadrant III tasks, and think about whether there is an opportunity to renegotiate deadlines or delegate them to someone else. Eliminate or reduce Quadrant IV tasks where possible, replacing them with an activity that restores your energy and wellbeing.

WORK IN SHORT, SHARP BURSTS TO OPTIMISE YOUR FOCUS AND PRODUCTIVITY

I have used the 'Pomodoro Technique' for the past few years, and I find that it works really well. The technique consists of working in short bursts of twenty-five minutes, followed by taking a five-minute break to optimise your productivity. The name of the technique is 'pomodoro' (Italian for 'tomato') because Francesco Cirillo, who developed the method, had a tomato-shaped timer that he used at university to time his twenty-five-minute bursts of work.[48]

I find this technique is great for ensuring that I get up and move around, rather than sitting at the computer for a long stretch at a time. I also find it useful for making progress on work that I simply don't want to do! I just need to do twenty-five minutes of it at a time – and that feels easier to commit to than completing the whole task in one go (which might require several hours of focused time and energy). Often, I find that I have broken through and made great progress in those twenty-five minutes, and that I want to keep going. Other times, I feel like I have made good progress but don't want to keep going or have something else I need to do. I then commit to working on that task for another twenty-five minutes the next day. I am *always* pleasantly surprised by what I can achieve in twenty-five minutes when I commit to a task. I am more likely to avoid distractions or to not defer my work when that timer is running, and I always feel better after having made progress instead of deferring my tasks to another day.

EXERCISE: TAKE CONTROL OF YOUR TIME BY WORKING IN SHORT, SHARP BURSTS TO OPTIMISE YOUR FOCUS AND PRODUCTIVITY

To take control of your time by working in short, sharp bursts to optimise your focus and productivity, complete this two-part exercise.

1. Reflection:
Consider your answers to these questions:

- How long can you sit and focus on a task before you get distracted and start checking emails, or engaging in activities that are not meaningful or value-adding?
- Are you mindful about taking short breaks and moving around – getting your body moving, mixing it up, and giving yourself much-needed breaks?
- Are there important tasks that need your attention and that will take up time and energy – but that you are just not getting to? Does it just feel too difficult to do them?

2. Action:
Give the Pomodoro Technique a go. Choose an important task and commit to working on it for twenty-five minutes. Set a timer and go! After twenty-five minutes, stop, and take a five-minute break that requires you to move around or do something else. Then, either return to the task and do another twenty-five minutes if you have the time available, or set it as a task to have another go at tomorrow. If you have time available between meetings or other commitments, consider chunking the time in your diary down into half-hour timeslots, working through your to-do list twenty-five minutes at a time. Reflect at the end of the day on how that worked for you by thinking about your answers to these questions:

- Did you make some progress on something that had previously felt stalled or had been hard to get to?
- Did your tasks take as long as you thought they would?
- Do you feel like you honoured your time and energy better than usual?
- Regardless of your responses to these questions, do you think you might try again tomorrow?

CHOOSE YOUR NUMBER ONE

James Clear, author of *Atomic Habits*, asks you to consider, when planning your day, what is the most important thing you need to do that day. Then do that, before anything else.[49] Your number one is a task that you choose as the first and most important task for your workday. It is something that you will prioritise above other work, and that you will commit to making progress on during your workday. A day when you make progress on your number one is a good day!

There are always things that will come up and get in the way of your progress. Of course. But prioritising your number one will increase your chances of completing, or at least working on, the task on that day. Think about the one thing that, if you completed or progressed it during your workday, would make you feel a sense of accomplishment. Once you've identified it, prioritise that task within the constraints of your workday. Think about getting up early to work on it or blocking out time to dedicate to that task. Try to avoid checking your emails and answering non-urgent phone calls, if possible, until you have completed or made progress on your number one.

When I am avoiding doing a task or something is not coming naturally, I might choose to make it my number one so that I commit to working on it before turning my attention to anything else. I combine strategies, like using the Pomodoro Technique and choosing my number one, to hack my way through and make progress. Rarely does the work involved ever feel as difficult as I expected it to when I was actively avoiding the task.

EXERCISE: TAKE CONTROL OF YOUR TIME BY CHOOSING YOUR NUMBER ONE

To take control of your time by choosing your number one, complete this two-part exercise.

1. Reflection:
Consider your answers to these questions:

- What task, if you made progress on it today, would make you feel the greatest sense of accomplishment, and like you have done work with meaning and purpose?
- What task is important and needs doing that you haven't been able to get to (or have been avoiding doing because it feels too difficult)?

2. Action:
When looking at your diary or to-do list for your workday, allocate a single task as your number one. Do your

very best to put that task first - and to avoid distractions, where possible, until you have made meaningful progress. Congratulate yourself if you complete the task or make progress. Be kind to yourself if, despite your best intentions, you are not able to get to it. Set it as your number one for tomorrow and try again.

LISTEN TO AUDIOBOOKS
Reading is something that has always brought me joy. I have a great imagination, and I can still remember how, when I was younger, I would get so caught up in stories that I would read into the wee, small hours. Somewhere along the way – when I was studying at university and then later, when I always had a growing pile of work-related reading to get through – I stopped reading for pleasure.

I felt like I didn't have the time to read and that it was a luxury of the past. When I was living with burnout, it just never seemed possible to have the energy or focus available to read. But as I started on my path to recovery from burnout, reading was one of the things that I had on my list of bucket fillers. I decided to start reading for pleasure again – but I still found making time for it a challenge, and when I did relax to read, I would inevitably fall asleep after getting through a couple of pages. (Not a bad thing – sleep is good – but reading wasn't happening.)

To prioritise my reading time, I started going to a book club with a group of girlfriends and I committed to reading a book every six weeks. That external motivation was helpful in keeping me on task and it was also a bucket filler connecting with my friends. I also discovered the miracle of audiobooks. I could listen to a book while driving home from the school run, while going for a walk, or even while cooking or doing housework (now that's my kind of multitasking). With audiobooks, I found that I could not only really get into the story, but that it was also an act of self-care, since it felt nurturing to have someone read to me.

Reflecting back, I've found that I've read more books in the past five years than in my lifetime so far. I always have something on the go – a mix of work-related and for-pleasure reads. Reading brings me joy, inspires me, takes me to other worlds, and gives me respite. And it doesn't feel like it's a drain on my time or energy – in fact, it's just the opposite.

EXERCISE: TAKE CONTROL OF YOUR TIME BY LISTENING TO BOOKS

To take control of your time by listening to books, complete this two-part exercise.

1. Reflection:
Consider your answers to these questions:

- Do you find it hard to find the time to read – or fall asleep after reading a few pages (or less!)?
- Do you love reading, yet find that it always seems to drop to the bottom of the list of things you need to do, becoming a pleasure you can indulge in only when things are less busy? If so, do you often find

yourself wondering whether that time of 'things being less busy' might never even come?

2. Action:
Try downloading an audiobook or subscribing to a podcast in an area of interest to you (personal or professional). Fit listening to your audiobook or podcast into the available moments in your days and evenings, and see how you feel as you get caught up in a story and realise you have given your brain a break from worry and stress.

3. GET PLAYFUL WITH TINY HABITS

One of the things I did early in my path to recovery from burnout was to consume TED Talks. I even binge-watched them at times! While doing this, I discovered a series of TED Talks called Life Hacks.[50] I watched them all, taking notes and then practising the key techniques they included. I realise that might seem a little OTT (over the top), but perhaps that isn't such a bad thing. I was determined to get myself and my life back on track, and I was going to try anything that might provide benefits. And guess what? Using the TED Talk Life Hacks *worked*.

At one point, I had a journal I used every day to track my progress on a whole set of hacks. It was effective. I still practise many of the following hacks – some daily, some every now and again. And if I'm going through a difficult time, or feel my energy waning and like my wellbeing is compromised, I know that I have these tools in my toolkit, and that I can recommit to them and use them to get me through.

PRIORITISE A SIMPLE GRATITUDE PRACTICE

At the end of each day, write down one thing you are grateful for that happened in the last twenty-four hours. At the start of each day, write down three things you are grateful for.

SMILE

Even if you are feeling really down – especially if you are feeling down, in fact – smiling or laughing out loud will actually make you feel better. Try it!

CARRY OUT SIMPLE ACTS OF SELF-COMPASSION

Here's an example. Place your hands on your heart and say something to yourself that you would say if it were a friend who was feeling how you are feeling at the moment.

PRACTISE POWER AND VICTORY POSES

Standing with your hands on your hips, with your legs shoulder-width apart, is the power pose. It can give you a quick boost of confidence and help you settle your nerves.

The victory pose is a natural stance when you are winning, in which you raise your arms above your head in a 'V' shape, just like people do as they cross the finish line in a race. You might not have just won a race, but you can get the same surge of good feelings by just doing the pose. Really! This pose can also be great for boosting your confidence when you're feeling nervous before giving a presentation, or walking into a tricky meeting or conversation.

WORK ON YOUR MENTAL AGILITY

Here's an example. In your head, count down from 100 to zero, skipping every seven numbers, so you go, '100, ninety-three, eighty-six, seventy-nine', and so on.

ENGAGE IN RANDOM ACTS OF KINDNESS

Think of something kind you can do for someone else and do it. This can be as simple as sending a message, letting them know that you are thinking of them, making a phone call to say hello, or sending a card in which you tell them why you are glad to have them in your life. No matter how challenging your circumstances are, sharing kindness with others will make you feel good.

These hacks we've reviewed are just a handful of strategies that I found helpful. There are many more, and I challenge you to find some hacks of your own. Get curious and look around for other strategies that can help you build your energy, and bring a little sense of ease and flow into your work and your life.

EXERCISE: GET PLAYFUL WITH TINY HABITS

To get playful with tiny habits, complete this two-part exercise.

1. Reflection:
Consider your answers to these questions:

- When you think about increasing your energy and

improving your wellbeing, does it feel too difficult or seem unachievable?
- Is it possible that you could adopt a tiny habit for as little as a few minutes a day and derive benefits? Is it worth giving it a shot?

2. Action:
Try out these simple hacks we've just covered and see how they make you feel. Consider creating a list of two or three and integrate them into your day for the next week.

WHAT WOULD YOU DO IF YOU HAD FUEL TO BURN?

There is so much to gain from filling your bucket and stemming the out-flows. Benefits include increasing your energy reserves so that you can keep turning up, improving your wellbeing, doing your best work, *and* living your best life. Another benefit is reducing the impact your low energy levels have on your ability to do the things that bring you joy and your capacity to engage meaningfully with the people who matter to you most.

Beyond these benefits, there are positive flow-on effects related to your health, wellbeing and life that result from many of the practices included. These are:

- Greater presence and mindfulness
- Less stress, and having a whole raft of tools to manage it better than ever before

- Increased joy and contentment in your everyday life
- Greater freedom and scope to consider new activities or to take on troubling problems instead of constantly treading water
- Meaningful progress in the direction of your goals and dreams

BURNOUT FACTS #5

WORK ROLES AND INDIVIDUAL FACTORS THAT INCREASE OUR RISK OF BURNOUT

As you may have discovered, specific work roles, plus a series of individual factors, put you at higher risk of burnout.

WORK ROLES IN WHICH WE ARE PARTICULARLY VULNERABLE TO STRESS AND DISTRESS

In specific work roles, we may have sustained exposure to stressful and distressing situations, including: illness and suffering, trauma, distress in those who are unwell and in their loved ones, a sense of helplessness and hopelessness when we are unable to relieve suffering, and death. Emotionally charged situations can be common in our work, and exposure to violence in the workplace is not uncommon in the health sector.

The level of stressors that are particular to each role, and the extent to which those stressors are sustained, is also an indication of risk. Long working hours and on-call roles are associated with a higher level of burnout. Specific roles and workplace settings with increased exposure to trauma and grief have also been identified. These include palliative care, hospices, emergency services and cancer care.

INDIVIDUAL CHARACTERISTICS THAT INCREASE OUR BURNOUT RISK

By now, it's not hard to see why burnout is such a problem in our health and social sectors. This final dimension explores the personal characteristics that increase an individual's risk of burnout.

This is what we know about people who are more prone to burnout. They often are:

- Women
- Younger health professionals, early in their career
- Midlife professionals juggling multiple roles outside of work, including caring for children, caring for elderly parents, working and planning for retirement
- People who have stress at home, such as financial concerns, ill health, carer responsibilities, relationship conflict, a lack of support, or an inability to carve out healthful downtime to nurture and recharge
- People who are experiencing conflicts between work and family
- People who are socially isolated and lonely
- People with high ideals and a tendency for perfectionism
- People who have an external locus of control (others are to blame)
- People with an avoidant coping style
- People with low self-esteem or sense of self-worth
- People who derive their sense of identity and meaning from work[51][52][53]

In looking at this list, it's hard to separate out where work and the rest of our lives start and end. This is a key challenge in purpose-driven work, where our sense of purpose and meaning can be intrinsically linked to our work.

The reality of the health and social sectors is that change is the norm, resources are stretched, demand is growing, and our population is ageing. This means that many needs remain unmet, and that some of the really intractable problems that we face require long-term engagement and intervention to achieve meaningful outcomes. Continued striving, innovation and transformation is the only way for us to make meaningful progress. In whatever role we are playing, we need to turn up in wholehearted service, so that we can do our very best each and every day that we are engaged in our work. We need to learn, grow and evolve, and we need to sustain our efforts over time. We dearly need to have energy in our reserves to take on this important work. Burnout cannot be accepted as inevitable.

A CAUTIONARY TALE

WITH A HAPPY ENDING: JUST START

Here's what happens when you take control and build your energy reserves.

No matter what Isabel achieved, her workload only seemed to grow as deadlines got closer and closer. Isabel found herself on that hamster wheel: working long hours had become the norm, and work responsibilities were noticeably and increasingly encroaching on her family life, diminishing her leisure time and affecting her personal relationships. Isabel found herself feeling emotional at work, an occurrence that increased in frequency over time and that really impacted her confidence.

Isabel recognised that this situation was no longer sustainable, which meant that she would have to make some changes. So, she started to deliberately catch herself whenever she engaged in negative self-talk. When she did that, she then tried to reframe her thoughts into useful and positive dialogue. Isabel chose to believe that, if she were to create clearer boundaries around her work, and to enjoy more time doing the things she loved with the people she loved, that her work would actually benefit. She told herself that she would have greater focus and productivity when she was working – and that she would, as a result, achieve just as much or even more than before.

Instead of working after dinner, Isabel reclaimed her evenings for downtime with her partner. She focused on increasing the duration and the quality of her sleep, and would not allow work to creep

into her thoughts or into her activities on non-workdays. She also started thinking about the things that brought her energy and joy, and tried to consciously find the time to do those things.

Nowadays, Isabel is working less and stressing less. She sleeps better and feels less like she is sacrificing the most important things in her life. She is enjoying more quality time with family, and feeling more consciously present and joyful in the simple moments with her children and partner. To her surprise, this change in her life has not even put a small dint in her output – and, when really major deadlines hit, Isabel has space in her week (which she barely had before) to do the extra work needed to meet the necessary requirements. She does this without resentment, as this is no longer the norm and she is not feeling compromised.

PART 3

COMMIT TO YOU AND PLAN FOR YOUR SUCCESS

Are you ready to make a commitment to you?

Have I convinced you that putting yourself and your needs first is the only way you can optimise and sustain your capacity to serve others?

Is it time to dispense with unhelpful beliefs that have held you back and that have made you hardwired for struggle?

Imagine routinely catching yourself when engaging in unhealthy self-talk or habits that are holding you back – and actively shifting them, reframing them, and stepping forward with a greater sense of ease and flow.

Are you ready for work *and* life to just not feel so difficult? And exhausting?

To regain your sense of self.

To reimagine your hopes and dreams.

To re-establish your connection with the purpose and meaning of your work, and then enjoy how that purpose and meaning spill over to and enrich all areas of your life.

To bring a bit of loving-kindness into your life so that you feel safe, protected, happy, peaceful, healthy, strong and at ease.

In this final part of the book, you will create a plan to get you there, and commit to a process in which you will accomplish all of this and more.

CHAPTER 5

PULLING TOGETHER YOUR PERSONAL IMPACT PLAN

'A goal without a plan is just a wish.'[54]

I love the term 'baby steps' as a metaphor for the slow, gradual building of skills and confidence towards walking, a skill that most of us have the good fortune to take for granted.

In its literal sense, 'baby steps' is the long, slow process a baby goes through while building strength and coordination, sitting up, crawling, pulling themselves up, and taking supported steps while holding onto furniture or holding onto someone's hand – until, one day, that first step is taken, often followed by a fall. Then there's another step, and then another, all of them followed with more stumbles along the way. But then, finally, the baby starts walking and enters a new phase with new capabilities and, literally, a different view of the world.

The metaphor of 'baby steps' works in a similar way to the process of taking control, restoring your wellbeing, and stepping forward into your best work *and* your best life.

Just like in this metaphor, your choice to take a different path away from burnout, and towards a sustainable path to your best work *and* best life, is a time of learning and evolution. You will look at yourself and at others in a different way. You will notice things that you previously weren't tuned into. You will try new things and learn a lot – about yourself and about the world around you. And, through a process of trial and error, you will let go of the things that have been weighing you down and holding you back, taking one step and then another and then another step forward. There is no question that there will be stumbles and frustrations along the way – but the insight, mindset and energy you will have gained in the process will make it easier for you to dust yourself off, get back up and keep on trying.

To carve this new path and implement the changes you need to get you there, you need a clear, concise and empowering plan that will enable you to focus your efforts and that will guide you along your pathway to wellness.

THE IMPORTANCE OF CREATING YOUR PERSONAL IMPACT PLAN

The simple act of taking the time to develop your personal impact plan allows you to set a clear intention to prioritise your wellbeing and to commit to 'better' (whatever 'better' looks like for you). Beyond a New Year's resolution or a single goal, this plan will include what matters most to you across all aspects of your life – and it will also be designed to build your reserves, so that you can ensure you are equipped to go the distance. Like the strategic plans developed within our workplaces, your personal impact plan will include one or more aspirational goals, your underpinning values, and actions that are specific, realistic and timed.

And like with any strategic plan, its development is just the starting point. It is in the implementation, the monitoring and tracking of progress, and the adjustment of the plan to respond to emerging issues, challenges or opportunities that the real progress happens. It's the creation of new routines, your reflection on progress, the celebration of successes, the noting of areas that need improvement, and refocusing and reprioritising that will be important to ensuring your success. This is the next level of your commitment to you.

You deserve the feeling of relief and joy that comes with taking control of your wellbeing.

Facing the truth of your situation and developing insight regarding its problems *without* daring to carve a new path forward can feel worse than the relative 'comfort' of staying right where you are now. This is where the plan comes in. Creating insight and facing your current truth is where you start – and daring to create a plan to get to 'better' is where you finish this process. Truth *and* dare (not or!).

You need to commit to the actions in your plan, and you need to make the effort to implement them. You need to be mindful, however, that you don't create more overwhelm while going through this process. Baby steps, remember.

Any action is better than none.

Facing the truth of your situation and developing insight regarding its problems *without* daring to carve a new path forward can feel worse than the relative 'comfort' of staying right where you are now. This is where the plan comes in. Creating insight and facing your current truth is where you start – and daring to create a plan to get to 'better' is where you finish this process. Truth *and* dare (not or!).

By using careful consideration, and applying some of the strategies you already use in your work to your own personal impact plan, you will create a better plan that is more likely to be effective.

Let's get started.

CREATING YOUR FIRST PERSONAL IMPACT PLAN

Follow these steps to pull together your personal impact plan for the coming year. While you do this, you might want to flick back through the book and consider the exercises you have completed. Then, complete these following sections to create your plan.

1. THEME:
Choose a theme for the coming year that will help keep you focused on and mindful of what you are trying to achieve. This theme should be a single word or a phrase that inspires you – that you include in your plan but that you also lock into your thinking as you progress through the year.

2. GOALS:
Set some goals for the coming year. Start with a brainstorm without limits, and then refine them down to no more than three goals. Less is better, clear is better. As you are developing these, think about what you want to achieve – *but also* think about how you want to feel. As you refine the wording of your goals, take your mind forward to one year from today. Ask yourself, 'If I have achieved this goal, will my life be better? Will I feel better? Will I feel a greater sense of ease and flow?'

3. VALUES:

Add in your core values. These are the principles that you will not compromise on in the coming year, and that will help you stay true to yourself. Again, start with a brainstorm and list all the values that resonate with you. There's a gazillion or so values lists online, if you want to look for some inspiration or ideas. Then, refine your list to a handful that resonate most strongly for you. Think about which of the values give you a sense of peace and flow whenever you implement them in your work and life. Think about the values that, if challenged or compromised, will make you feel most out of alignment.

4. STOP:

What are you going to stop doing? Give yourself permission to knock items off your to-do list. Also, be mindful of the drainers that you can control. Think about self-talk, responsibility you are taking on for others, uncomfortable situations or conversations you might be avoiding, and ways of lessening your load.

5. START:

What are you going to start doing? Think about your bucket fillers – things you can start doing to fill that bucket, restore some balance in your life, build your energy reserves, and shift your mindset in a positive way. Also think about your bucket drainers – things you can start doing that will reduce the drain on your reserves, like saying no, setting boundaries, negotiating timeframes, and using new techniques to manage your time and energy.

6. KEEP:

What are you going to keep doing? What are the activities or practices that you derive benefits from, that work for you, and that you will ensure you keep doing? Think about new habits you have adopted, and activities that bring you joy and build your energy.

Here are some more options. Maybe it's what you have started by reading this book and developing this plan. Maybe you're going to keep putting yourself first. Or continue to focus on your energy and wellbeing. Or keep learning and growing, testing out new ways of thinking and acting. Keep working out what works for you in this moment. And the next moment. And the next moment.

7. YOUR ACTION LIST:
Here's where you get real and commit to very tangible actions with a timeframe. It's where you create a few clear, simple actions with a deadline that you commit to completing them by. I would again start with a bit of a brainstorm of a set of possible actions.

I would recommend thinking about two timeframes: one month from now and three months from now. These more immediate timeframes help you keep your plan and action list manageable, and also give you the scope to revisit your plan monthly and quarterly, setting new actions based on the progress you have made. Consider the possible actions you identified as you completed the experiences in the book, and think about the eighty-twenty rule. Which are the ones that will provide you with the greatest impact or relief in the short term? Which are the ones that will give you more time and energy, increasing your capacity further? Then select the actions that you feel will give you the most benefit.

8. CAPTURE YOUR PLAN AND HAVE IT HANDY FOR INSPIRATION AND REFLECTION:
If you create your plan by hand, make sure you date it and take a

photo of it so you can save it on your computer and phone, and have it on hand if you ever wanted to reflect on it. If you create it as a digital document, make sure you save it with the date it was created. Pin your plan up somewhere where it will be a visual reminder of the commitment you have made to yourself as you move forward. As you update the plan with new actions over the course of the year, be sure to save the older versions so you have a record that you can reflect back on over time.

9. CREATE RITUALS THAT WILL HELP ENSURE YOU STAY ON TRACK:
This might involve reviewing your plan, celebrating your progress, and sharing your success along the way. There are some tips for you to consider as you implement and track your progress, as well as repeat the planning process over time.

IMPLEMENTATION AND TRACKING PROGRESS

- ☑ Set a meeting appointment (for you with you) to review your progress at the end of each month.
- ☑ At the end of each month, reflect on your progress and set your actions for the coming month.
- ☑ At the end of each quarter, set a new set of actions for the next quarter.
- ☑ At the end of each year, reflect on each of the sets of actions and your progress.
- ☑ Each step of the way, acknowledge and celebrate what you have achieved, and consider sharing those achievements with someone you love.

- ☑ Always, always, always be gentle and kind to yourself when it comes to the things you haven't yet achieved, and think carefully about whether they need to go on the next list or whether they've been superseded by another item. If so, let them go. (Remember: this is supposed to make life easier, not harder.)

At the end of the first year:

- ☑ Consider redoing the exercises in Chapter 2 and comparing your results to those of the previous year.
- ☑ Celebrate where you can see and feel progress happening, and think about the year ahead and what you need to focus on.
- ☑ Think about creating a new plan and restarting the action-planning process for the coming year.

CONCLUSION:

MY HOPES FOR YOU

I hope there has been something or – better still – multiple things in this book that resonated with you.

I hope that you have taken some time to put yourself first, and for that to be the case because you believe that you deserve to do so.

I hope that you have thought about and worked through the steps in this book so that you can reclaim your energy and your sense of self – and re-chart an easier path ahead.

I hope that this path brings you greater ease and flow, wellness and joy.

I hope that you enjoy great success and more far-reaching impact through your work.

I hope that you have truly worked out a plan that takes you a few baby steps closer to your best work *and* your best life, where you:

- Do more than survive but thrive
- Lead a life that you will reflect back on one day without regret
- Have tended to the things that matter to you the most

- Have created a legacy that you can be proud of
- Have lived well

And finally, as a leader, I hope that you will model good practices in self-care and balance for those you work with. That you become a role model for 'better'. That you inspire others to do the same. That you become part of the change we so dearly need in our health and social sectors.

Some closing words of inspiration from Maya Angelou:

> *'If I am not good to myself, how can I expect anyone else to be good to me?'*[55]

As a leader, I hope that you will model good practices in self-care and balance for those you work with. That you become a role model for 'better'. That you inspire others to do the same. That you become part of the change we so dearly need in our health and social sectors.

ENDNOTES

PART I: A SUSTAINED STATE OF CRISIS WE HAVE NORMALISED

INTRODUCTION

1   Oxford University Press (2020). Burnout. On Lexico.com, available at: https://www.lexico.com/definition/burnout

2   National Aeronautics and Space Administration (NASA) (2020). *50 years ago: "Houston, we've had a problem"*. Available at: https://www.nasa.gov/feature/50-years-ago-houston-we-ve-had-a-problem

3   Freudenberger HJ. (1974). Staff burn-out. *Journal of Social Issues*, 30: 159-165.

4   Kane L. (2020). Medscape national physician burnout and suicide report 2020: The generational divide. Available at: https://www.medscape.com/slideshow/2020-lifestyle-burnout-6012460

5   Kane L. (2019). Medscape national physician burnout and suicide report 2019. Available at: https://www.medscape.com/slideshow/2019-lifestyle-burnout-depression-6011056

6   Imo UO. (2017). Burnout and psychiatric morbidity among doctors in the UK: a systematic literature review of prevalence and associated factors. *BJPsych Bulletin*, 41:197-204.

7   Beyond Blue (2019). The National Mental Health Survey of Doctors and Medical Students. Available at: https://www.beyondblue.org.au/docs/default-source/research-project-files/bl1132-report---nmhdmss-full-report_web

8   McHugh MD, Kutney-Lee A, Cimiotti JP, Sloane DM and Aiken LH. (2011). Nurses' widespread job dissatisfaction, burnout, and frustration with health benefits signals problems for patient care. *Health Aff*, 30(2): 202-210.

9   Hansen V and Girgis A. (2010). Can a single question effectively screen for burnout in Australian cancer care workers? *BMC Health Services Research*, 10: 341-345

10   Girgis A, Hansen V and Goldstein D. (2008). Are Australian oncology health professionals burning out? A view from the trenches. *Eur J Cancer*, 45(3): 393-399.

11   Safe Work Australia (2020). Available at: https://www.safeworkaustralia.gov.au/topic/mental-health#snapshot-of-claims-for-mental-health

12   Kane L. (2020). Medscape national physician burnout and suicide report 2020: The generational divide. Available at: https://www.medscape.com/slideshow/2020-lifestyle-burnout-6012460

13   Kane L. (2019). Medscape national physician burnout and suicide report 2019. Available at: https://www.medscape.com/slidshow/2019-lifestyle-burnout-depression-6011056

14   Beyond Blue (2019). The National Mental Health Survey of Doctors and Medical Students. Available at: https://www.beyondblue.org.au/docs/default-source/research-project-files/bl1132-report---nmhdmss-full-report_web

CHAPTER I: IT'S TIME TO TAKE CONTROL, AND IT STARTS WITH YOU

15   Ware B. (2019). *The top five regrets of the dying: A life transformed by the dearly departing*. Second Edition. Hay House Inc. United Kingdom.

16   World Health Organization (2020). Burn-out an "occupational phenomenon": International Classification of Diseases. Available at: https://www.who.int/mental_health/evidence/burn-out/en/

17   Maslach C and Leiter MP. (2017). New insights into burnout and health care: Strategies for improving civility and improving burnout. *Medical Teacher*, 39(2):160-163.

18   Baigent M and Baigent R. (2018). Burnout in the medical profession: not a rite of passage. *The Medical Journal of Australia*, 208(22):471-473.

19   McHugh MD, Kutney-Lee A, Cimiotti JP et al. (2011). *Health Aff (Millwood)*, 30(2):202-210.

20   De Keyrel A. (2017). *Is nurse burnout on the rise? Startling statistics on nurse wellbeing*. Online article available at: https://www.mededwebs.com/blog/well-being-index/is-nurse-burnout-on-the-rise-startling-statistics-on-nurse-well-being

21   Tavella G and Parker G. (2018). *Extinguished and anguished: What is burnout and what can we do about it?* Online article available at: https://newsroom.unsw.edu.au/news/health/extinguished-and-anguished-what-burnout-and-what-can-we-do-about-it

22 Kurapati R. (2019). *Burnout in healthcare: A guide to addressing the epidemic.* Independently published.

PART 2: GETTING PRACTICAL AND ZOOMING IN ON YOU

CHAPTER 2: INSIGHT: FACE YOUR TRUTH

23 Cambridge University Press (2020). Insight. In Cambridge Dictionary, available at https://dictionary.cambridge.org/dictionary/english/insight

24 Helder C. (2016). *Useful belief: Because it's better than positive thinking.* John Wiley and Sons Australia Ltd. Australia.

25 Rath T and Clifton DO. (2004). *How full is your bucket?* Gallup Press. Canada.

26 Crocker L and Crocker C. (2019). *The patient advocate handbook: How to find and use your voice in health care.* Balboa Press. United States.

27 Gilbert E. (2015). *Big magic: Creative living beyond fear.* Bloomsbury Publishing. United Kingdom.

28 World Health Organization (2020). Burn-out an "occupational phenomenon": International Classification of Diseases. Available at: https://www.who.int/mental_health/evidence/burn-out/en/

29 Kane L. (2020). Medscape national physician burnout and suicide report 2020: The generational divide. Available at: https://www.medscape.com/slideshow/2020-lifestyle-burnout-6012460. Viewed April 2020.

30 Kane L. (2019). Medscape national physician burnout and suicide report 2019. Available at: https://www.medscape.com/slideshow/2019-lifestyle-burnout-depression-6011056

31 Beyond Blue (2019). The National Mental Health Survey of Doctors and Medical Students. Available at: https://www.beyondblue.org.au/docs/default-source/research-project-files/bl1132-report---nmhdmss-full-report_web

CHAPTER 3: MINDSET: ENABLE CHANGE

32 Dweck C. (2012). *Mindset: Changing the way you think to fulfil your potential.* Robinson. United Kingdom.

33 Bialylew E. (2018). *The happiness plan.* Affirm Press. Australia.

34 Diamond D. (2016). How to make a difference when times are tough.

TEDxRainier. Available at: https://www.youtube.com/watch?v=YWyo1qlNd3g

35 Gilbert E. (2015). *Big magic: Creative living beyond fear*. Bloomsbury Publishing. United Kingdom.

36 Helder C. (2016). *Useful belief: Because it's better than positive thinking*. John Wiley and Sons Australia Ltd. Australia.

37 Bell R. (2016). *How to be here*. William Collins. United Kingdom.

38 Vilfredo P. (1896-1897). Cours d'Économie Politique Professé a l'Université de Lausanne, Vol. I, 1896; Vol. II, 1897.

39 Koch R. (2004). *Living the 80/20 way*. Nicholas Brealey Publishing. United Kingdom.

40 Bono G, Sender JT. (2018). How gratitude connects humans to the best in themselves and in others. *Research in Human Development*, 15:224-237.

41 Garcia-Rill E. (Ed.). (2015). *Waking and the reticular activating system in health and disease*. Elsevier Inc. United States.

42 Maslach C and Leiter MP. (2017). New insights into burnout and health care: Strategies for improving civility and alleviating burnout. *Medical Teacher*, 39(2): 160-163.

CHAPTER 4: ENERGY: BUILD YOUR RESERVES

43 *Alice in Wonderland*. (1951). [Motion picture]. Geronimi C, Luske H, Jackson W, Directors. United States. Walt Disney Productions. This film is based on the works of Louise Carroll: *Alice's Adventures in Wonderland* (1865) and *Through the Looking-Glass* (1871).

44 Zaccaro A, Pairulli A, Laurino M et al. (2018). How breath-control can change your life: A systematic review on psycho-physiological correlates of slow breathing. *Frontiers in Human Neuroscience*, 12:353. doi: 10.3389/fnhum.2018.00353.

45 US Department of Health and Human Services (2018). *Physical Activity Guidelines for Americans, 2nd edition*. Washington, DC: US Department of Health and Human Services.

46 Huffington A. (2014). *Thrive: The third metric to redefining success and creating a happier life*. WH Allen. United Kingdom.

47 Covey S. (1989). *The seven habits of highly effective people*. Free Press. United States.

48   Cirillo F. (2018). *The pomodoro technique: The life-changing time management technique*. Random House. United Kingdom.

49   Clear J. (2018). *Atomic habits: An easy and proven way to build good habits and break bad ones*. Random House. United Kingdom.

50   TED Talks: Life Hacks. Available at: https://www.youtube.com/playlist?list=PLJTXSMas_Be1ObYMReRwp6S84E4pwlKsk

51   Gallagher R. (2013). Compassion fatigue. *Canadian Family Physician*. 59:265-268.

52   Baigent M and Baigent R. (2018). Burnout in the medical profession: not a rite of passage. The *Medical Journal of Australia*, 208(22):471-473.

53   McFadden R. (2017). Workplace stress is reaching toxic levels in social sector. Online article available at: https://probonoaustralia.com.au/news/2017/05/workplace-stress-reaching-toxic-levels-social-sector/

PART 3: COMMIT TO YOU AND PLAN FOR YOUR SUCCESS

CHAPTER 5: PULLING TOGETHER YOUR PERSONAL IMPACT PLAN

54   de Saint-Exupéry A. (1943). *The Little Prince*. Harcourt, Brace and World. New York, United States.

CONCLUSION: MY HOPES FOR YOU

55   Maya Angelou. Available at: https://www.facebook.com/MayaAngelou/posts/if-i-am-not-good-to-myself-how-can-i-expect-anyone-else-to-be-good-to-me-maya-an/10154475030879796/

www.ingramcontent.com/pod-product-compliance
Lightning Source LLC
Chambersburg PA
CBHW061200070526
44579CB00009B/75